SKILLS FOR THE FIRST-TIME SUPERVISOR

Douglas Gordon
Career Solutions Training Group
Paoli, PA

VISIT US ON THE INTERNET
www.swep.com
www.thomson.com

SOUTH-WESTERN
™
THOMSON LEARNING

Australia • Canada • Mexico • Singapore • Spain • United Kingdom • United States

SOUTH-WESTERN
THOMSON LEARNING ™

Quick Skills: Skills for the First-Time Supervisor
By Career Solutions Training Group

Vice President/Executive Publisher
Dave Shaut

Team Leader
Karen Schmohe

Project Manager
Laurie Wendell

Production Manager
Tricia Matthews Boies

Editor
Alan Biondi

Executive Marketing Manager
Carol Volz

Channel Manager
Nancy Long

Marketing Coordinator
Linda Kuper

Manufacturing Coordinator
Kevin Kluck

Cover Design
Tippy McIntosh

Copy Editor
Karen Davis

Compositor
Career Solutions Training Group

Printer
The Mazer Corporation

Betty Barrett
Instructor
Northern Kentucky Technical College
Covington, Kentucky

Kevin J. La Mountain
Dean of Career and Student Services
DeVry Institute of Technology
Phoenix, Arizona

Nicola Pidgeon
Coordinator, Business and Community Services
Schenectady County Community College
Schenectady, New York

Dr. Madelyn Schulman
Assistant Administrator
Office of School-to-Career Transition Services
New York City Board of Education
Brooklyn, New York

Brian Sporleder
Dean of Instruction
Bryant and Stratton College
Milwaukee, Wisconsin

13 East Central Avenue, Paoli, PA 19301
Telephone: 1-888-299-2784 • FAX: (610) 993-8249
E-mail: cstg@bellatlantic.net • Website: www.careersolutionsgroup.com

Doris Humphrey, Ph.D.: Project Manager
Jane Galli: Production Editor

WORKSHOP 1

Mara is a young carpenter with Alwood Construction Company. She works on a team that does interior woodwork on custom-built homes. She's proud of her work, and her supervisor, Ryan, frequently praises her efforts.

One morning she gets a message to report to the firm's vice president, and this worries her. Did she do something wrong? If there's a problem, why didn't she hear about it from Ryan?

She enters the office of Mr. Algozzine, who is standing behind his desk. "Yes, sir?" Mara says softly. "You wanted to see me?"

Brusquely the vice president motions her to a chair. "I hear you turn a nice banister," he tells her. "In fact, I've looked at your work myself, and I like it. Your jobs are done on schedule, and the customers are happy. What I want to know is, could you turn out a whole house like that?"

"An entire house? Well, I've done all kinds of woodwork—cabinets, baseboards—and with enough time, I'm sure I—"

"I don't mean by yourself," Mr. Algozzine interrupts. "I mean as

crew chief. We're transferring Ryan to a project out of town, and he says you're the one to take over, even though you're the youngest on the crew."

Mara is amazed and pleased, but still very nervous. Herself a crew boss? Her head spins.

"Since you don't have supervisory experience, you'll have to learn fast," Mr. Algozzine goes on. "But we believe you can do it. You'll get a 15 percent raise, by the way."

Mara pulls herself together and expresses her thanks for the confidence the firm has shown in her. But as she leaves the vice president's office, she is thinking, "Wow! How am I going to handle this?"

What's Inside

In these pages, you will learn to:

- appreciate the reasons for being a supervisor .... p. 4
- describe the functions of a supervisor .... p. 6
- improve your time management skills .... p. 10

Workshop 1: Being a Supervisor

③

Workshop Introduction presents a short story relevant to the workshop.

What's Inside begins each lesson with clear learning outcomes.

Activities challenge learners to apply information from the workshops to real workplace situations.

ACTIVITY 1.2

Rating Yourself on Supervisory Functions

1. For each of the supervisory functions you have read about, decide how much you would enjoy performing it. That is, would you really like organizing work and assigning tasks, or would you find that job unpleasant? Rate your likely enjoyment on a scale of 1 to 5, with 5 being the highest. Circle the appropriate number.

Setting goals and planning	1	2	3	4	5
Organizing work and assigning tasks	1	2	3	4	5
Controlling quality and schedules	1	2	3	4	5
Making decisions, solving problems	1	2	3	4	5
Motivating employees	1	2	3	4	5
Instructing and coaching	1	2	3	4	5
Evaluating personnel	1	2	3	4	5
Handling change and conflict	1	2	3	4	5

2. Now do a similar rating, but base it on your estimate of your current level of skill at each function. That is, if you think you're excellent at planning and setting goals, give yourself a 5 in that category. If you believe you'd be terrible at that task, give yourself a 1. Do the same for all eight tasks.

Setting goals and planning	1	2	3	4	5
Organizing work and assigning tasks	1	2	3	4	5
Controlling quality and schedules	1	2	3	4	5
Making decisions, solving problems	1	2	3	4	5
Motivating employees	1	2	3	4	5
Instructing and coaching	1	2	3	4	5
Evaluating personnel	1	2	3	4	5
Handling change and conflict	1	2	3	4	5

3. Now compare your answers to questions 1 and 2. What can you learn from the comparison? For instance, do you find a high correspondence between what you would like and what you think you're good at? If so, would raising your skill level for certain tasks change your attitude toward those tasks?

_____

_____

	Often	Sometimes	Never
1. If I feel my job is important, I'm not too anxious about my title or my official status.	☐	☐	☐
2. I enjoy doing many types of work.	☐	☐	☐
3. I can cope with frequent changes in my environment.	☐	☐	☐
4. I like working at a fast pace.	☐	☐	☐
5. When I take on a project, I have lots of creative ideas.	☐	☐	☐
6. I can work independently, taking a project from idea to completion.	☐	☐	☐
7. I'm good at working as a member of a team.	☐	☐	☐
8. My work shows that I care about my organization's reputation.	☐	☐	☐
9. I'm not afraid of risks, but I know how to analyze and minimize them.	☐	☐	☐
10. I'm good at solving unexpected problems.	☐	☐	☐
11. I pay close attention to financial matters.	☐	☐	☐
12. I'm effective in all aspects of leadership, such as communicating a vision, providing direction, and building a healthy work climate.	☐	☐	☐

How many times did you check "Often"? The more checks you placed in that column, the more prepared you are right now for an entrepreneurial type of business. But don't worry if some or all of your answers fell into the other two columns. Skills for an entrepreneurial organization can be learned, and this book will help you do just that.

Self Check
provides short
self-assessment on
the topic of
supervision.

The Sandwich Technique

Many successful supervisors conduct evaluation interviews with a method known as the sandwich technique. First, they stress the employee's strengths and accomplishments. Then they note any problems or weaknesses. Finally, they return to positive remarks, showing how the employee can remedy the problems and build on his or her strengths. By "sandwiching" the bad news between more positive remarks, the supervisors avoid overemphasizing the negative, and they convey their own solid support for the employee.

Tips for Setting Goals

- ✓ If possible, involve your staff members in the process of setting goals for the team. The goals will mean more to them if they take part in creating them.
- ✓ Make the goals challenging but realistic—that is, not too easy, but not impossibly hard.
- ✓ Define the goals specifically, in measurable terms. Rather than saying, "We want to increase our production," specify, "We want to increase our production by 15 percent over the next six months."
- ✓ Write your goals down. Doing so will help you clarify them.
- ✓ Be sure that all employees understand the goals and why they are important.

Information Boxes
highlight interesting
facts, findings, and
trends in the area of
supervision.

GETTING CONNECTED

Browse the online resources and articles at Monster.com's Leadership Center:

http://leadership.monster.com/

What do you see that relates to your own needs as a supervisor?

As another option, check the articles you find by entering the search term *supervision* or *supervisor* at Smartbiz.com:

http://www.smartbiz.com/

See if any of the suggestions will help you develop your skills in the areas you have identified as being your weakest.

Getting Connected suggests web sites to visit for additional information on supervision.

Did You Know highlights interesting facts, findings, and trends in supervision.

> Leadership: The art of getting someone else to do something you want done because he wants to do it.
>
> —President Dwight D. Eisenhower

Quotations Statements from authors, leaders, and celebrities add relevance, humor, and motivational messages.

Did you know

When faced with a tough decision, many supervisors believe they can rely on their instinct or intuition. Sometimes they're right, especially if they are experienced managers with a deep understanding of human nature.

The foundation of good intuition, however, is prior knowledge and thought. If your "sixth sense" warns you that a certain choice is wrong, it's because your brain is processing relevant information from your past experience. Consequently, your intuition will improve if you work to establish a strong base of knowledge.

WORKSHOP WRAP-UP

- Advantages of a supervisory position include not just salary, status, and power, but also the joy of meeting challenges and the sense of personal accomplishment.
- Supervisors perform many functions, including setting goals and planning, organizing the work, controlling performance, making decisions, motivating workers, instructing and coaching employees, evaluating personnel, and handling change and conflict.
- Time management is a fundamental skill for an effective supervisor.

Workshop Wrap-Up provides a recap of the key points from the workshop.

CONTENTS

Y ou're very good at the work you do. The managers of your organization recognize your ability, and in due time they promote you. Now you're a boss yourself, and you're supervising others—a great achievement!

This familiar scenario may apply to you. If so, your knowledge of the job, plus the work skills you've already developed, will help you lead others to superior performance. Soon you'll discover, however, that understanding how to do the work yourself is only a fraction of your job as a supervisor. There's so much else you need to know. For instance, how do you encourage others to be as committed to the work as you are? How do you instruct employees and correct their mistakes without making them resent you?

If you're in a typical U.S. firm, your task as a supervisor is made even more challenging by the diversity of the workforce. People of Hispanic, African American, and Asian heritage make up more than 25 percent of the civilian labor force, and the percentage continues to increase. Women hold close to half of all jobs, and that proportion too is rising. Overall, the American workforce is older and better educated than ever before, but there are large gaps between the high-skilled and the low-skilled.

What do these numbers mean? They suggest that, as a supervisor, you'll probably be responsible for leading people who are very different from you, not only in their degree of training, but also in their schooling, their heritage, and their cultural outlook. In this situation, you can't just "wing it." You need the skills of a supervisor.

This book will help you identify and develop those skills. To begin, try the self-assessment on the next page. For each statement, mark the response that best applies to you.

> " I will pay more for the ability to deal with people than for any other ability under the sun. "
>
> —John D. Rockefeller
> Business Leader

INTRODUCTION

	Often	Sometimes	Never
1. I like facing new challenges at work.	❏	❏	❏
2. I don't mind assuming responsibility.	❏	❏	❏
3. I adapt well to different situations.	❏	❏	❏
4. I manage my time efficiently.	❏	❏	❏
5. I'm good at organizing tasks and delegating them to other people.	❏	❏	❏
6. I can plan out a project successfully from beginning to end.	❏	❏	❏
7. I'm good at solving tough problems and making difficult decisions.	❏	❏	❏
8. I know how to get other people motivated.	❏	❏	❏
9. I'm a good, careful listener.	❏	❏	❏
10. I can critique people's work without offending them.	❏	❏	❏
11. I can handle rapid change without getting upset.	❏	❏	❏
12. I'm good at settling conflicts between others.	❏	❏	❏

If you checked "Sometimes" or "Never" for any of the above items, this book will help you improve in those areas. If you checked "Often" in every instance, you may still find that you have more to learn.

Even experienced supervisors need to keep learning in order to meet new challenges.

WORKSHOP 1

Mara is a young carpenter with Alwood Construction Company. She works on a team that does interior woodwork on custom-built homes. She's proud of her work, and her supervisor, Ryan, frequently praises her efforts.

One morning she gets a message to report to the firm's vice president, and this worries her. Did she do something wrong? If there's a problem, why didn't she hear about it from Ryan?

She enters the office of Mr. Algozzine, who is standing behind his desk. "Yes, sir?" Mara says softly. "You wanted to see me?"

Brusquely the vice president motions her to a chair. "I hear you turn a nice banister," he tells her. "In fact, I've looked at your work myself, and I like it. Your jobs are done on schedule, and the customers are happy. What I want to know is, could you turn out a whole house like that?"

"An entire house? Well, I've done all kinds of woodwork—cabinets, baseboards—and with enough time, I'm sure I—"

"I don't mean by yourself," Mr. Algozzine interrupts. "I mean as crew chief. We're transferring Ryan to a project out of town, and he says you're the one to take over, even though you're the youngest on the crew."

Mara is amazed and pleased, but still very nervous. Herself a crew boss? Her head spins.

"Since you don't have supervisory experience, you'll have to learn fast," Mr. Algozzine goes on. "But we believe you can do it. You'll get a 15 percent raise, by the way."

Mara pulls herself together and expresses her thanks for the confidence the firm has shown in her. But as she leaves the vice president's office, she is thinking, "Wow! How am I going to handle this?"

What's Inside

In these pages, you will learn to:

A Step Up

Like Mara, people who are good at their jobs often find themselves being promoted to supervisory positions. Sometimes, as in Mara's case, the change comes as a surprise. But even when you've been expecting it, the new position can seem daunting. Some of the employees under your leadership may be older and more experienced than you are. Moreover, you will now be judged not just by your own performance, but by the performance of all the people you are overseeing.

Given the difficulties of a supervisory position, some people decide they don't want the promotion. They'd rather do more limited jobs, take the paycheck, and go home without extra worries. The first issue to address in this workshop, then, is why you should want to be a supervisor.

Why Be a Supervisor?

There are some obvious advantages to being a supervisor:

♦ **Higher salary and better benefits.** By long-established practice, those who manage other people are paid more—often considerably more—than those who manage only tasks or machines. They may also receive superior benefit packages—better insurance, more vacation time, and so forth.

> " To build any cathedral requires at least one person with a higher purpose. "
>
> —John McCormack
> *Self-Made in America*

♦ **Increased status.** Supervisors have higher status in the company than base-level workers. They are treated with greater respect. Perhaps they have "perks" such as parking spaces close to the building.

♦ **Power.** Supervisors have power over others—over the jobs they do, the way they spend their time at work, and often over whether they are promoted or fired.

♦ **Career advancement.** A supervisory position is typically the first step in a rise up the corporate ladder.

Most people enjoy increased status and power, and everyone likes a higher salary. If these are your only reasons for becoming a supervisor, however, you may be ill suited to the job. Good supervisors enjoy their positions for more subtle reasons, such as these:

♦ **The joy of meeting challenges.** Successful supervisors take pleasure in facing and solving new problems. They enjoy jobs that aren't routine.

♦ **The chance to help the organization meet its goals.** As a supervisor, you can have a major impact on your department's and your firm's success.

♦ **A greater sense of accomplishment in one's work.** As your job becomes more significant to the overall performance of the firm, you feel an expanded sense of pride and accomplishment. This feeling can raise your self-esteem and influence your entire attitude toward life.

You've probably known one or two supervisors who didn't care much about meeting challenges and helping the organization reach its goals. They focused only on selfish benefits such as money and power. What did you think of them as supervisors?

ACTIVITY 1.1

A Supervisor You Have Known

Think of a person you consider a successful supervisor. This could be someone for whom you have worked, or it could be a school or training leader. Once you have identified such a person, answer the following questions about him or her.

1. Why do you think this person was given a supervisory position by the organization? Was it just seniority, or did the person have special qualities and talents?

   _____

   _____

   _____

2. Do you think this person enjoys being a supervisor? Why or why not? That is, what aspects of the job does the person especially like or dislike?

   _____

   _____

   _____

3. Would you enjoy doing this person's job? Why or why not?

   _____

   _____

   _____

4. What major personality traits do you share with this supervisor you have identified? In what ways are you different?

   _____

   _____

   _____

Functions of a Supervisor

Now that you've begun to think about why you might want to be a supervisor, it's time to consider the functions for which a supervisor is responsible. These can vary, of course, from company to company and from one supervisory position to another. Commonly, however, a supervisor's work includes the tasks described in the following list. For each task, note the typical questions that the supervisor has to answer.

1. **Setting goals and planning.** Whether the supervisor is in charge of a small team or a larger group, one task is to establish goals for the work and then devise a plan to achieve those objectives. Say the team is producing computer motherboards. In the short term, how many boards should it produce in a day? In the long term, what are the ways to improve output and quality? What are the steps for reaching these goals? When and how should each step be taken?

2. **Organizing the work and assigning tasks.** Say there are ten tasks to be done. How will they be divided? How many people will be assigned to each? Which people? A supervisor makes these choices.

3. **Controlling work performance.** After planning and organizing, the supervisor must set up a control process to ensure that the work actually gets done according to plan. What checks will ensure that a project stays on schedule? How will the final product be inspected for quality? How will costs be controlled?

Did you know

For many years, educators have emphasized the role of teachers' expectations in student achievement. When teachers expect their students to succeed, the students often do. If teachers think their students are doomed to fail, however, the students often live up to those expectations.

The same kind of self-fulfilling prophecy has been found in the business world. Supervisors who set high goals and expect high performance from their subordinates generally get better results than those who expect little. The goals have to be realistic, of course, and the employees have to know that their efforts are appreciated.

4. **Making decisions and solving problems.** From the planning stage forward, the supervisor is constantly making decisions and solving problems that arise. Often the supervisor has to cope with unexpected situations. Say the production line snags and one key employee is sick, but the schedule still has to be met—how can this difficulty be handled?

5. **Motivating employees.** Employees who don't care about the work will do a poor job. How does the supervisor encourage them to care? What incentives can the supervisor offer?

6. **Instructing and coaching.** Typically the supervisor is highly skilled at some or all of the tasks the employees are doing. But how can the supervisor convey these skills to others? How much instruction is needed? When and how should it be done?

7. **Evaluating personnel.** The supervisor may be directly responsible for hiring, promoting, and firing employees. Even if those decisions are someone else's responsibility, the supervisor will have to provide personnel evaluations on which the decisions will be based. What are fair criteria for judging an employee's performance? Should Margie be given a higher rating than Joe?

8. **Handling change and conflict.** This function is inherent in all of the other supervisory tasks, but it is so important that it deserves special attention. In any work team there are internal changes— employees come, employees leave, people learn new skills, people develop different relationships. Moreover, today's work environment is continually evolving because of changes in technology, company mergers, and so on. The supervisor must handle all these changes in such a way that the team remains efficient.

> " No organization is so excellent, no team so unified, no business so successful that it is immune to internal conflict. "
>
> —Kenneth Kaye
> *Workplace Wars and How to End Them*

And when conflict erupts—a commonplace occurrence if employees are stressed by rapid change—the supervisor has to manage it. Say the new computer system has disrupted internal communications, and Joe is mad at Margie because he thinks she failed to distribute an important notice. How can this flare-up be managed? Who will say what to whom?

The division of time among these various supervisory functions changes as a person rises through an organizational hierarchy. A first-level supervisor, such as a production team leader or an office manager, may spend the most time on controlling, instructing, and motivating. At higher levels in the organization, managers spend more of their time in planning, organizing, and evaluating. Decision making and the management of change and conflict are major tasks at every level.

In later workshops, you'll learn specific skills relevant to all of these functions. Right now, Activity 1.2 will help you decide which functions you most need to work on.

How Closely Should You Supervise?

You know how annoying it is to have someone constantly looking over your shoulder. Imagine that your significant other asks you to help plant flower bulbs in the garden. The job is a simple one that takes only half an hour, but on three separate occasions she or he comes by to check on whether you're doing the job right. At the final interruption you exclaim, "Do you think I'm totally incompetent? And how can I do the job if you keep pestering me?"

Supervisors may inspire similar reactions if they try to exercise extremely close control over routine tasks that are being handled by capable, confident employees. A good supervisor adapts the supervisory techniques to the nature of the job and the characteristics of each individual on the staff.

In deciding how closely to supervise, there are two basic questions to consider:

♦ How much direct supervision does the employee need?
♦ How much direct supervision does the employee want?

Of course, the answers to these questions often conflict. The employee may want more or less supervision than he or she actually needs. You have to find a way to balance concern for the task with consideration of the employee's long-term development and morale. If the immediate task is all-important, the employee's feelings may have to be wounded a bit. If the task is minor, you may decide to allow the employee to make mistakes and learn from them.

Rating Yourself on Supervisory Functions

1. For each of the supervisory functions you have read about, decide how much you would enjoy performing it. That is, would you really like organizing work and assigning tasks, or would you find that job unpleasant? Rate your likely enjoyment on a scale of 1 to 5, with 5 being the highest. Circle the appropriate number.

Setting goals and planning	1	2	3	4	5
Organizing work and assigning tasks	1	2	3	4	5
Controlling quality and schedules	1	2	3	4	5
Making decisions, solving problems	1	2	3	4	5
Motivating employees	1	2	3	4	5
Instructing and coaching	1	2	3	4	5
Evaluating personnel	1	2	3	4	5
Handling change and conflict	1	2	3	4	5

2. Now do a similar rating, but base it on your estimate of your current level of skill at each function. That is, if you think you're excellent at planning and setting goals, give yourself a 5 in that category. If you believe you'd be terrible at that task, give yourself a 1. Do the same for all eight tasks.

Setting goals and planning	1	2	3	4	5
Organizing work and assigning tasks	1	2	3	4	5
Controlling quality and schedules	1	2	3	4	5
Making decisions, solving problems	1	2	3	4	5
Motivating employees	1	2	3	4	5
Instructing and coaching	1	2	3	4	5
Evaluating personnel	1	2	3	4	5
Handling change and conflict	1	2	3	4	5

3. Now compare your answers to questions 1 and 2. What can you learn from the comparison? For instance, do you find a high correspondence between what you would like and what you think you're good at? If so, would raising your skill level for certain tasks change your attitude toward those tasks?

_____

_____

A Fundamental Skill: Time Management

Deficiencies in any of the skills you read about in the preceding section can cause you trouble when you become a supervisor. Later workshops in this book will address each of those skills and help you build your competence. First, however, you should think about one fundamental matter that will affect all your

efforts: the way you manage your time. When you're in charge of a group, it may seem that you have *less* control over your own time than ever before. While you're trying to plan and organize, your team members may interrupt you repeatedly with questions. Small crises may steal most of your time. If one person is out sick, for example, you may spend all day trying to make up for that absence, and in the process none of your other work will get done.

The higher you advance in an organization, the more important it is to manage your time wisely. Here are some tips:

♦ Prioritize the tasks you have to do. Distinguish between those that are important and those that are merely pressing. That is, make sure that important long-term tasks are not neglected in the rush to deal with small emergencies.

♦ Control interruptions. Let people know when to approach you and when not to interrupt what you're doing.

♦ Learn to say "no" when your own supervisors ask you to take on more tasks than one human can handle.

♦ Learn to delegate effectively. (You will read more about this skill in Workshop 3.)

♦ Keep your work space organized and neat so that you don't lose time in looking for documents, supplies, or tools.

♦ Practice a once-past-the-desk approach to memos, reports, and correspondence. As soon as you receive an item, screen it and decide what to do with it: for instance, read it now, file it, circulate it, or throw it away. Don't get bogged down in useless information or waste time sorting the same pieces of paper again and again.

♦ Keep a daily to-do list and a weekly personal planning calendar to help you prioritize your tasks and budget your time.

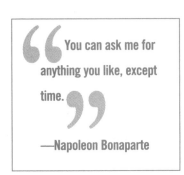

> You can ask me for anything you like, except time.
>
> —Napoleon Bonaparte

Assessing Your Time Management

For each of the statements listed below, decide how well it applies to you. Answer as honestly as you can. Rate yourself on a scale of 1 to 5 by circling the appropriate number.

	Not True of Me				Very True of Me
1. I feel overwhelmed by the amount of information I have to deal with.	1	2	3	4	5
2. Every day, no matter how many urgent problems arise, I make some progress toward long-term goals.	1	2	3	4	5
3. I can't trust people to do things right unless I check on them constantly.	1	2	3	4	5
4. I can find my tools and papers right away when I need them.	1	2	3	4	5
5. Because I know what I have to do, I don't bother keeping a calendar.	1	2	3	4	5
6. One of my handiest tools is the wastebasket.	1	2	3	4	5
7. It seems like I can't stop people from interrupting me.	1	2	3	4	5
8. Each night, I write a list of what I have to do the next day, in order of priority.	1	2	3	4	5
9. People are always imposing on me, giving me tasks that aren't really my job.	1	2	3	4	5
10. However busy I am, I always have time for rest and recreation.	1	2	3	4	5

To calculate your total score for this exercise, first *reverse* the scores for the odd-numbered items. That is, if you wrote a 5 next to the first item, make it a 1; if you wrote a 4, make it a 2. (A 3 stays the same.) Now add up all the numbers. The maximum score is 50. The closer you came to 50, the more likely you are to manage your time wisely as a supervisor.

Look back at the items on which you had the poorest scores. What can you do to improve your skills and habits in those areas?

_____

_____

_____

_____

_____

_____

_____

Browse the online resources and articles at Monster.com's Leadership Center:

http://leadership.monster.com/

What do you see that relates to your own needs as a supervisor?

As another option, check the articles you find by entering the search term *supervision* or *supervisor* at Smartbiz.com:

http://www.smartbiz.com/

See if any of the suggestions will help you develop your skills in the areas you have identified as being your weakest.

WORKSHOP WRAP-UP

- Advantages of a supervisory position include not just salary, status, and power, but also the joy of meeting challenges and the sense of personal accomplishment.
- Supervisors perform many functions, including setting goals and planning, organizing the work, controlling performance, making decisions, motivating workers, instructing and coaching employees, evaluating personnel, and handling change and conflict.
- Time management is a fundamental skill for an effective supervisor.

Rajiv is visiting his mentor, Tracy, in the county's Parks Department. "You know," Rajiv sighs, "this job is twice as hard as I thought."

Until recently, Rajiv handled the children's programs at the Nature Center in the county's largest park. Two months ago, however, he was put in charge of all the Center's programming, supervising a staff of five.

"What's the problem?" asks Tracy.

"Well," Rajiv says, "I'm having trouble with my staff—the people who are supposed to listen to me. It seems like each employee has his or her own little kingdom, and when I try to coordinate the programs—even to make sure, for instance, that birdwatchers aren't disrupted by 20 third graders tramping past—all I get is resentment."

"What kind of leadership are you giving your people?" Tracy asks. "Are you just telling them what to do? Are you having meetings, asking for suggestions?"

"I've tried everything," Rajiv insists. "First, I called a meeting. I pointed out that our programs have expanded so much that we need a rational plan to coordinate them. Then I laid out my plan and asked for comments. Nobody offered objections, so I thought that settled the matter. A week later, I realized nobody was paying attention to my plan."

"What did you do then?"

"I called another meeting and lectured them about being team players. That made people mad. Now I'm going around to each employee personally, asking for ideas and comments, but they're holding back, as if they don't trust me. What did I do wrong?"

"It sounds like you've tried different managerial styles," Tracy says, "and staff members are confused about who you really are."

"I'm the same person I always was," Rajiv muses. "Maybe I need to show them that."

What's Inside

In these pages, you will learn to:

Leadership Style

As Rajiv discovered, formal authority doesn't translate automatically into leadership. You can be named a supervisor, but the mantle of a true leader is one you have to earn. Unfortunately, there isn't one prescribed way for a leader to act. In fact, the many varieties of leadership style have long been a hot topic for researchers.

You may have heard of the Theory X and Theory Y approaches to leadership, originally defined by Douglas McGregor:

♦ *Theory X* leaders believe that workers are naturally lazy and undisciplined. To control workers, they use an autocratic (dictatorial) style of leadership, issuing direct orders and inviting no feedback.

♦ *Theory Y* leaders, in contrast, believe that workers are self-motivated and enjoy responsibility. As a result, Theory Y leaders are more open and democratic.

Often the democratic Theory Y approach is referred to as *participative* leadership, because it invites employees to become part of the decision-making process. Of course, there are many degrees of employee participation. (See the diagram below.) One supervisor may encourage input from employees but insist on retaining the right to make the final decision. Another supervisor may go along with whatever the majority of the group decides. Whatever the degree of employee input, the participative manager usually takes care to explain decisions and build the workers' trust.

What the Supervisor Says	Amount of Employee Participation
"Let's discuss the options and then take a vote."	██████████████████████
"I'm open to suggestions. Feel free to speak up."	█████████████
"Does anyone have problems with our procedures?"	████████
"Do it this way."	██

Other researchers have studied leadership in terms of the leader's primary focus. In this respect, also, two contrasting types have been identified:

♦ *Task-oriented leaders.* Some leaders are concerned mainly with the task to be accomplished. They concentrate on making sure that employees do the job in the best way possible.
♦ *Relationship-oriented leaders.* Other leaders are more concerned with keeping employees satisfied and harmonious, so that they function as a well-organized team. These leaders want to build good relationships throughout the work group.

Although the correspondence is not absolute, task-oriented leaders tend to be rather autocratic, and relationship-oriented leaders usually allow more democratic, participative decision making.

If you think about it, you can see that different styles of leadership have both advantages and disadvantages. Look at the following lists, and see if you can think of other items to add.

Advantages of an Autocratic, Task-Oriented Style

♦ Decisions can be made quickly.
♦ Responsibility for each decision is clear-cut.
♦ Workers know exactly what is expected of them.

Disadvantages of an Autocratic, Task-Oriented Style

♦ When a decision is imposed from above, workers may have little understanding of its importance.
♦ Staff members may lose interest and motivation.
♦ When not told exactly what to do, employees used to autocratic leadership are often at a loss.
♦ Little attention may be paid to individuals' needs.
♦ In the long run, workers may resent their bosses.

> Leadership: The art of getting someone else to do something you want done because he wants to do it.
>
> —President Dwight D. Eisenhower

Advantages of a Participative, Relationship-Oriented Style

♦ People share their ideas, talents, and experiences, a process that often leads to wiser decisions.

♦ Employees become more creative when given freedom to do so.

♦ Smart, dedicated employees will tend to feel that their talents are being used and appreciated.

♦ Employees are often happier overall.

♦ People work harder to implement their own ideas than they would if just following orders.

♦ Given greater freedom and responsibility, employees tend to grow in their degree of competence, increasing the organization's human resources.

♦ Employees need less direct supervision, so the leader has more time for long-range planning.

Disadvantages of a Participative, Relationship-Oriented Style

♦ It often takes a lot of time and energy to involve everyone in a decision.

♦ Sometimes the group will never reach a clear conclusion.

♦ Some employees don't like to take responsibility for decisions.

♦ Employees may become confused about their responsibilities.

♦ Part-time and low-skilled employees may have little to contribute to decision making.

♦ If the participative style leads to less direct supervision, inexperienced workers may make too many mistakes.

♦ A supervisor can use participative decision making as an excuse for procrastinating or for avoiding strong action.

Your Own Leadership Style

For clues about your own natural leadership style, decide whether you agree or disagree with the statements below. For each item, circle the most appropriate number.

	Strongly Disagree				Strongly Agree
1. A leader should set clear, specific goals for subordinates.	1	2	3	4	5
2. The leader's number-one task is to raise productivity as high as possible.	1	2	3	4	5
3. Supervisors should keep close tabs on all important aspects of the team's work.	1	2	3	4	5
4. A supervisor should aim for respect from employees, not friendship.	1	2	3	4	5
5. An effective leader can delegate small tasks, but nobody else can make the major decisions.	1	2	3	4	5
6. Quick decisions are essential in today's economy.	1	2	3	4	5
7. People are happiest when they know exactly what is expected of them.	1	2	3	4	5
8. The average person likes to avoid genuine responsibility.	1	2	3	4	5
9. Personal fulfillment is nice, but most people shouldn't expect to find it at work.	1	2	3	4	5
10. Meetings are often a waste of time.	1	2	3	4	5

Now calculate your total score by adding up the numbers you circled. The maximum is 50. The closer you came to 50, the more you tend toward an autocratic, task-oriented style of leadership. The lower your score, the more you probably favor participative, relationship-oriented leadership.

Note that a "high" score on this activity is not necessarily good. Autocratic leaders can have a lot of trouble in today's business environment. Whatever your natural style, the next section will help you learn how to adapt it to the situation.

Three Rules of Thumb

In general, the trend today is toward participative leadership. Management is much less autocratic than it was several decades ago. Workers expect their opinions to be heard and respected. Few managers would contend that employees are naturally lazy or incapable of thinking for themselves.

In fact, many managerial experts advise supervisors to become "facilitators" and "coaches" rather than "bosses." That is, instead of telling employees what to do, these advisers say, you should coach them to develop their own skills for analyzing a task and deciding how to approach it.

To be a successful supervisor, then, you'll have to be sensitive to your employees' needs and desires, and you'll probably have to use a leadership style that is at least moderately participative. In later workshops you'll work on specific skills for these purposes. First, though, there are three rules of thumb that can help you become an effective leader:

- Be yourself.
- Be flexible.
- Adapt to the situation.

Be Yourself

As a supervisor, it doesn't help to pretend to be somebody you're not. You can't just learn how to play the role of a supervisor like an actor memorizing a part. If you try spouting lines that you don't really believe, your employees will recognize your pretense.

Therefore, you need to find a leadership approach that reflects your own basic nature. Try to find a combination of task-oriented and relationship-oriented elements that suits your personality and your beliefs about human nature. Draw ideas from everything you read and everyone you observe, then put them all together into your own synthesis. After all, you are unique as a person, so why shouldn't you be unique as a supervisor?

Be Flexible

Just as you will be unique as a supervisor, every person working for you will be unique as an employee. No two subordinates will think or act exactly alike. Therefore, though you may have general rules that apply to all, you need to be

> " A given leader need not be *either* a task-type leader *or* a human relationships-type leader. A particular leader may well tend to engage in both activities, in one combined leadership pattern. "
>
> —David R. Hampton, Charles E. Summer, and Ross A. Webber
> *Organizational Behavior and the Practice of Management*

Knowing Yourself

Classic advice for success in any endeavor is to "play to your strengths"—that is, to take advantage of what you do best. In leadership, though, you can sometimes even take advantage of your weaknesses.

Jeff M. is a young choir director from the Midwest who has led both student and adult vocal groups. Though he is a mild-mannered, soft-spoken person, the frustrations of choir directing build up in him over the course of a season, and sooner or later, he loses his temper and flies into a tirade at his choir members. Jeff's secret is that he knows he has this tendency, and therefore he uses it to his—and the choir's—advantage. As much as he can, he times his explosion for the particular day or week when the choir members most need a chewing out.

This story is not a recommendation for losing one's temper. It does indicate, though, that self-understanding is a big plus for a leader. The better you understand yourself, the more you can use your personality traits to advance your goals.

flexible enough to respond to different needs and abilities. For example:

♦ Each employee will have a different type or level of expertise.
♦ Some employees will need more direct instruction than others.
♦ Some subordinates will accept criticism better than others.
♦ Some people need firm schedules, while others don't.
♦ Some people work best under pressure; others rebel when you pressure them.
♦ Some people function best in groups. Others need to work alone.

The more you can accommodate the idiosyncrasies of the people working for you, the better supervisor you will be.

Adapt to the Situation

The effectiveness of a particular leadership style often depends on the circumstances. Typically, for instance, a participative, relationship-oriented style is useful in situations like the following:

♦ A new problem calls for a creative approach.
♦ Employees are experienced, capable, and well motivated.
♦ Knowledgeable employees are available to act as leaders on certain aspects of a project.

In contrast, a more autocratic, task-oriented approach might be useful in situations like these:

- A crisis has occurred, and a decision is needed immediately.
- Team members are new at working together and unsure of their roles.
- Employees lack the experience and skills to accomplish their tasks without direct guidance.

You'll also find that many situations involve emotional issues. Imagine that you inherit the leadership of a work crew from a previous supervisor who was extremely unpopular. Overall, the work is being done well, but the authority of the supervisor's position has been undermined. In this case, you may want to begin by concentrating on building relationships with your team, showing that you're a fair, understanding person who can be trusted.

Now imagine a slightly different situation. Resentment of the previous supervisor has led to open rebellion, the team is doing terrible work, and the upper-level managers are impatient for quick improvement. In this instance, you may have to get tough before you can show your friendliness.

> " There is no one best style of leadership that consistently leads to high levels of performance. There are too many complex relationships in leadership to make this possible. "
>
> —Andrew D. Szilagyi, Jr.
> *Management and Performance*

Some researchers believe that a work team typically goes through distinct phases, with a different leadership style appropriate for each. For instance, Paul Hersey and Ken Blanchard have described four stages of leadership related to a team's level of "maturity":

- *Telling.* A new team needs a lot of direction, so the supervisor must be task-oriented and willing to give explicit instructions.
- *Selling.* As the team gains experience, the supervisor tries to "sell" ideas through persuasiveness rather than orders.
- *Participating.* When the team approaches maturity, the supervisor begins to behave more like a participant than like a "boss."
- *Delegating.* Finally, when the team is fully mature, the supervisor can delegate many leadership responsibilities to other team members.

Your own work teams may not correspond exactly to these stages. The general point, however, is that you should use all your experience, your reasoning power, and your knowledge of human nature to analyze the situation in which you and your employees find yourselves. Then you can decide which leadership approach best suits your goals.

Taking Charge

Imagine that the leader of this class or seminar becomes ill. You are suddenly promoted to lead the group through the rest of this workshop and the remaining ones. How are you going to handle it? Answer the following questions:

1. How will you show the group that you were the right choice as leader? That is, what will you do to earn the group's respect and trust?

   _____

   _____

   _____

   _____

2. How will your style of leadership differ from that of the current leader? Give specific examples of things you would do or not do.

   _____

   _____

   _____

   _____

3. What would be your most difficult problems as leader of the group?

   _____

   _____

   _____

   _____

4. Overall, would your leadership style be more autocratic or more participative than the current leader's? How and why?

   _____

   _____

   _____

   _____

Qualities of a Good Leader

In addition to studying leadership styles, researchers have examined the personalities of effective leaders. The studies show that successful leaders tend to share a number of personality traits or qualities.

It's important to realize that these qualities don't add up to a single "personality type." Leaders are too varied to fit a single type. However, it's useful to know that the following traits are common among people who gain success as leaders:

♦ Self-confidence and positive thinking
♦ Willingness to accept responsibility
♦ Initiative
♦ Assertiveness
♦ Strong desire for achievement
♦ Decisiveness
♦ Energy
♦ Persistence
♦ Honesty
♦ Courage
♦ Reliability and trustworthiness
♦ High degree of organization
♦ Creativity
♦ Tact and sensitivity to the needs of others
♦ Fairness
♦ Tolerance of frustration and pressure
♦ Versatility and willingness to adapt to new situations
♦ Skillfulness in communication

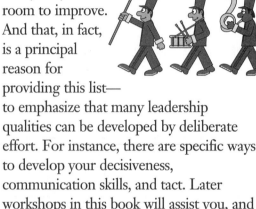

Of course, none of us is perfect in these qualities. Everybody has room to improve. And that, in fact, is a principal reason for providing this list— to emphasize that many leadership qualities can be developed by deliberate effort. For instance, there are specific ways to develop your decisiveness, communication skills, and tact. Later workshops in this book will assist you, and you can help yourself by constantly assessing your performance and analyzing how to improve in the future.

Did you know

Actions speak louder than words, the proverb says. Similarly, many management theorists believe that the best thing a leader can do is to set a good example.

If you are conscientious, dedicated to the job, and enthusiastic, those qualities will tend to rub off on subordinates. If you're open and responsive to reasonable criticism, you'll encourage your employees to follow suit. If you are fair, you'll create an environment of fairness. If you take pleasure in your work, you'll help to spread enjoyment around you.

Leadership Qualities

Think of a successful leader you have known or read about. It could be someone in business, sports, politics, or any other field. Answer the following questions about this person.

1. Of the leadership qualities listed in the preceding section, name two or three that you believe were most important for the success of the leader you have chosen. Why and how were they important? (If there are qualities *not* on the list that you think were even more important for this leader, feel free to comment on those.)

_____

_____

_____

_____

_____

_____

2. What were the leader's most notable weaknesses? For instance, are there any qualities in the list that your leader did *not* exhibit? Or did he or she have any other personality traits that created difficulties?

_____

_____

_____

_____

_____

_____

3. From your analysis of this leader, what conclusions can you draw for your own success as a supervisor?

_____

_____

_____

_____

_____

_____

GETTING CONNECTED

For help in assessing your own leadership qualities, check out the following web sites:

"Am I a Good Leader?" by Steven Reid:

http://www.globalnode.com/users/stevenr/quiz/leader.htm

"Leadership Assessment Tool" by InterLink:

http://www.interlinktc.com/assessment.html

"Innovative Leadership Assessment" by Chart Your Course International:

http://www.chartcourse.com/articleassess.htm

If you identify potential defects in your qualities as a leader, don't be discouraged. Instead, take those areas as challenges that you can work on. Draw up a plan for self-improvement.

WORKSHOP WRAP-UP

- Leadership styles vary from autocratic, task-oriented approaches to participative, relationship-oriented techniques. The trend today is toward participative styles.
- Three rules of thumb for effective leadership are: be yourself, be flexible, and adapt to the situation.
- Some of the typical qualities of successful leaders are self-confidence, decisiveness, creativity, tact, and skillfulness in communication. Characteristics like these can be developed with conscious effort.

Grace began at the health clinic as a secretary/receptionist, and she did very well. Recently, when the clinic expanded, she was named office manager, in charge of all the nonmedical staff. So far, she has found the new job difficult and very stressful.

This morning is typical. As she is helping Liya solve a problem with appointment schedules, Dr. Andrews bursts out of the back room complaining that she can't find any cotton swabs. "Are we out of swabs?" she demands. "How can we run short of something so basic? Who's keeping track of supplies?"

"I'm trying to," Grace answers, "but I have so much else to do, I hardly have time to think."

"You have four people working for you," Dr. Andrews points out. "Can't someone take a weekly inventory? You don't have to do it yourself. Just see that I get some swabs, please, before I start tearing up shirts."

As Dr. Andrews stomps off, Liya signals that Grace should take a phone call. "Another billing mistake," she whispers. The billing is being handled by Yuri, who is a reliable and conscientious employee but, unfortunately, new to the bookkeeping software the clinic uses. Because Grace trusted him, she didn't realize he was having trouble until complaints started pouring in.

Grace takes the phone and manages to calm the irate patient, who was charged twice for one procedure. Then she notices that Dr. Andrews has reappeared, holding two boxes of cotton swabs. "Found these in a cabinet," the doctor says, and then adds sympathetically, "Grace, I'm sorry I snapped at you. But there's got to be a better way of organizing the work around here and keeping things under control. Have you made any kind of plan? Think about this, and let's talk tomorrow."

What's Inside

The Core Functions

In the scenario you've just read, can you identify Grace's problems? If you think back to what you read in Workshop 1 about the functions of a supervisor, you'll see that she was struggling with three functions in particular:

1. By trying to do too much herself, Grace was falling short in her duty to *organize the work and assign tasks.* Surely somebody on her staff could have kept a weekly count of basic supplies like cotton swabs, and Grace would then have had more time for tasks of greater importance.

2. By letting Yuri do the billing with software he didn't understand, Grace failed to *control work performance.* As a supervisor, she needed to be more aware of the quality of work done by her subordinates.

3. Finally, we can suppose that, in her struggle to keep up with urgent matters, Grace gave little attention to *setting goals and planning.* If she had set clear goals for her staff and devised a plan to reach them, she might have prevented some of the problems that cropped up. A plan would have helped her realize, for example, that a regular inventory was needed.

These three functions can be considered the core duties of a supervisor—the most essential tasks you will have to handle. That's why this workshop is called "Three Essential Tasks." If you don't manage these tasks well, you're not likely to succeed. In the following sections, you'll gain knowledge and skills that will help you handle these crucial supervisory functions.

Setting Goals and Planning

You may suppose that planning and goal setting are relevant mainly for the top managers of large corporations. Sure, Bill Gates has goals and plans for Microsoft, but if you're supervising a small team or department, what's the point? The goal is just to get the job done as well as possible, you may argue, and the plan is to work hard—isn't that enough?

Sorry, the answer is no. No matter how small the staff you are supervising, you need goals and plans. The following sections will show you why.

Why Set Goals?

When you play a sport, do you ever aim for a certain level of performance? Let's say you're on a softball team, and today you have a game against your chief cross-town rivals. Will you set a team goal of winning

> It's essential to have a grip, a clear understanding, of what your values and priorities are. Without a clear set of values, one decision is as good as another.
>
> —Alvin Toffler
> Author of *Future Shock* and *The Third Wave*

the game? Personally, will you set a goal of, say, at least one hit in three at-bats? If you play second base, will you aim to make zero errors in the field?

If you care about the game, you'll almost certainly establish some goals for yourself and your team. Doing so helps boost your achievement. Rarely has a championship been won by a team that didn't aim to finish first. Successful teams, and successful players on those teams, set high goals for themselves.

The same is true at work. Goals tell you where you're going, and they are excellent tools for motivating yourself and others. As a supervisor, you can hope that your employees all have personal goals that they try to meet, but for the team as a whole, it's up to you to initiate the goal-setting process.

Your goals may include raising productivity and improving schedules. They may involve helping your staff

members learn new skills. Perhaps increasing customer satisfaction is a major goal for you. In some cases, your own boss may charge you with meeting certain goals, but you should still extend and interpret those objectives in your own way. For example, if your boss says, "Your team needs to improve quality control," you can set an objective of reducing errors by a definite amount within a certain time period.

Tips for Setting Goals

- ✓ If possible, involve your staff members in the process of setting goals for the team. The goals will mean more to them if they take part in creating them.
- ✓ Make the goals challenging but realistic—that is, not too easy, but not impossibly hard.
- ✓ Define the goals specifically, in measurable terms. Rather than saying, "We want to increase our production," specify, "We want to increase our production by 15 percent over the next six months."
- ✓ Write your goals down. Doing so will help you clarify them.
- ✓ Be sure that all employees understand the goals and why they are important.

Why Plan?

Have you ever thought it would be nice to learn Italian? Or have you wanted to buy an old sports car and refurbish it? All of us have dreams of things we'd like to do sometime. And those dreams remain just that—mere pictures in our minds—unless we make plans to accomplish them.

The same is true of your goals at work. They will be only pipe dreams unless you set up definite steps for reaching them. Moreover, like Grace in the scenario at the beginning of this workshop, failure to plan can expose you to all sorts of crises. Too many mistakes will be made, and people will be working at cross-purposes. You'll find yourself spending huge amounts of time and effort coping with problems that wouldn't have arisen if you'd worked out a sensible plan beforehand.

Guidelines for Planning

Here are some guidelines for effective planning:

1. **Make time for planning.** You may feel you're so rushed that you don't have time to plan. But unless you make time, the situation will never improve!

2. **Clarify your priorities.** Which of your goals are most important? Which tasks are most urgent? Plan to allocate your resources where they are most needed.

3. **Divide your tasks into small steps.** If you're planning to raise production by 10 percent, what specific steps are involved in doing so?

4. **Determine the best order of the steps; put first things first.** Many managers go wrong by trying to accomplish a task before they take care of prerequisites. For example, you can't speed up a production line unless the employees have been trained to work faster.

5. **Set a timetable for implementing each step of your plan.** Choose a realistic date for accomplishing the overall objectives; then work backward from that date to set a date for each of the steps.

6. **Put your plan in writing.** Again, writing helps you clarify your thoughts, and you'll want to refer to the details of your plan at later stages.

7. **At periodic intervals, evaluate the progress and make necessary adjustments.** Your plan may get off track if you don't monitor it. Often, in fact, it's a good idea to establish checkpoints as part of the plan itself. You'll read more on this subject later in this workshop.

Assessing Your Planning and Goal Setting

For each statement below, check the answer that best applies to you.

	Often	Sometimes	Never
1. When faced with a major task, I make a point of setting aside time to plan it before I start.	❏	❏	❏
2. I know how each of my tasks fits into my overall goals.	❏	❏	❏
3. I write out my plans on paper or on my computer.	❏	❏	❏
4. I define my goals in measurable terms so that I can check on my progress.	❏	❏	❏
5. I approach a large task by dividing it into small steps.	❏	❏	❏
6. Before rushing into things, I think about what I need to do first.	❏	❏	❏
7. When someone gives me a big deadline, I establish my own intermediate deadlines for separate parts of the task.	❏	❏	❏
8. I have to work hard to meet my goals, but they are all within reach.	❏	❏	❏
9. As I carry out a plan, I check to see how it is working, and then I make adjustments as needed.	❏	❏	❏
10. My planning allows me to concentrate on the most important things I have to accomplish.	❏	❏	❏

If you checked "Often" for every item, you may already be a good planner and goal setter. If so, think about how you can convey your goals and plans to people working for you.

If some of your answers were "Sometimes" or "Never," study those items and make a plan—yes, a plan!—for self-improvement.

Organizing Work and Assigning Tasks

Imagine that you're preparing a five-course meal for two dozen friends. You can't possibly do all the cooking yourself by the time the guests arrive—you need help! So four of your friends offer to pitch in. They arrive in your kitchen all at once, bumping into each other in their haste. Three of them start making pies when you really need assistance with the main course. To get the dinner prepared, you have to take charge. You need to determine an efficient way to divide up the work.

The same is true in your job as a supervisor. Whatever your line of business—and whether or not your subordinates already have clearly defined jobs—you'll face many decisions involving who should do what and when.

Recognizing When to Delegate

You've heard the old saying, "If you want a job done right, do it yourself." Many new supervisors follow this rule all too often. In their zeal to see the job done perfectly, they try to carry too great a load themselves. As a result, they become too harried to do anything right, and they have no time for effective planning.

Recognize that if you're the captain of your troop, you can't also be the lieutenant, the sergeant, and the corporal. This doesn't mean that you should act like a big shot who is too important for menial chores. Rather, it means that you should organize your own workload, and everyone else's, to serve the priorities you identified in your planning.

In general, a task can be delegated if:

♦ Someone else on your team has the skills and knowledge to handle it.
♦ You can explain the guidelines for performing the task.
♦ There is enough time for a subordinate to take over and become familiar with the task.
♦ Afterward, you will be able to judge whether the task was done correctly.

Tips for Effective Delegation

There are two basic rules for delegation that virtually everyone grasps:

1. Match tasks to the individual talents of your employees.
2. Check that no one has too much or too little to do.

Those points sound obvious, but they mean that you must be sensitive not only to the nature of the tasks to be done, but also to each employee's talents and needs.

Two other rules of delegation are not so widely recognized:

1. Whenever possible, delegate a whole job rather than just a fraction of it.
2. Along with the job itself, delegate as much authority and responsibility as possible. That is, allow the employee to make his or her own decisions, command resources, and take credit for the outcome.

This second pair of guidelines cannot be stressed enough. By delegating entire jobs with full authority and responsibility, you give your subordinates "ownership" of their work. This increases their interest and motivation.

Here are several further tips that can help you delegate tasks effectively:

♦ Explain each task fully, including the reasons for doing it and the criteria for performing it well.

♦ State deadlines clearly.
♦ Anticipate problems that employees are likely to face, and advise them how to cope.
♦ Provide any necessary training in advance.
♦ Monitor progress regularly, but don't keep looking over everyone's shoulder.
♦ If an employee needs support or assistance along the way, offer it promptly and graciously, without blaming the person for requiring help.

GETTING CONNECTED

For more information and tips on delegation, you can enter the phrase *effective delegation* in your favorite web search engine, such as Google:

http://www.google.com/

or AltaVista:

http://www.altavista.com/

Browse through the articles, book titles, and courses that the search turns up. What themes are common to all the advice on delegation? What ideas do you find that are most relevant for you in particular?

What's a Better Way?

For each of the following situations, point out what is wrong and explain how the supervisor could have handled the matter more appropriately.

1. Fred is unhappy because his supervisor has asked him to fill out a new form each week. The form requires him to list projects that are behind schedule and explain what the problems have been. Fred already has too much paperwork, and he doesn't see the point of doing more.

   _____

   _____

   _____

   _____

2. Jamie has to take the end-of-month inventory herself. Last month, she tried delegating the task, but the employee got confused and didn't do it right.

   _____

   _____

   _____

   _____

3. Noah's boss asked him to take over a project midstream, when it was already a mess. Despite what Noah thought were heroic efforts on his part, the project failed, and now it seems Noah is catching the blame. He is angry at his supervisor for putting him in that position.

   _____

   _____

   _____

   _____

4. Loretta's boss asked her to order a dozen copies of a book on supervision but didn't provide a source. She added that chore to her list, but in the crush of other duties, she didn't get to it for two weeks, and now the boss is cross because the books haven't arrived in time for a course he plans to teach.

   _____

   _____

   _____

Controlling Work Performance

Controlling work performance involves three basic steps:

1. Checking the performance: for example, monitoring schedules and quality and measuring output.
2. Comparing the performance to the original plan or to other established criteria.
3. Making the necessary adjustments to fix any shortcomings.

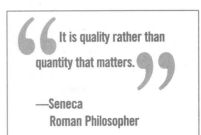

Controlling is a natural follow-up to planning and organizing the work. Your best arrangements may come to nothing if you don't monitor the performance. Good control procedures help you identify and correct mistakes, and they may give you early warning when the work starts to deviate from your plan.

What Is Controlled?

Typical control procedures involve any or all of the following:

- Quality
- Quantity
- Schedules
- Costs
- Inventory

As a supervisor, you will also need to monitor and evaluate your employees, so your control system should allow you to check these elements as well:

- Performance of teams
- Performance of individuals
- Whether employees are on time and work the scheduled number of hours
- Employees' motivation and attitudes toward the job
- Employees' mutual cooperation
- Problems affecting staff morale

Controlling as a Process

Controlling should be a regular process, not a haphazard, hit-or-miss affair. Often the control procedures are built into the plan itself. That is, the plan specifies certain checkpoints at which you'll determine whether the project is on schedule, whether costs are within budget, and so forth.

The particular tools you use in the controlling process depend on the type of work and the information you need to acquire. You may use one or more of these common techniques:

- Standardized forms on which the employees record crucial data
- Computerized data files
- Regular progress reports (written, oral, or e-mail)
- Group meetings at which employees report on the status of their projects

> ❝ It is quality rather than quantity that matters. ❞
>
> —Seneca
> Roman Philosopher

To speak of controlling as a process may make it sound terribly mechanical, like an automatic system that has little to do with people. In fact, it's just the opposite. Often, for a supervisor of a small staff, a crucial part of controlling is simply getting out among the employees, talking to them, finding out what's going on and what problems they're having. Formal status reports and data entries can be deceptive unless you're truly in touch with the daily work.

Whatever forms and systems you use, it is vital to inform employees about the control standards. People have to know what is expected of them. Moreover, they should know *why* it is expected, so that they can see you're not being arbitrary.

In enforcing the controls, you also need to strike a balance between firmness and fairness. Don't let a major project go wrong because you're afraid to criticize. On the other hand, don't berate someone for an insignificant deviation from your original scheme. Keep your priorities and the company's needs clearly in mind.

? Did you know

The controlling process helps you identify problems and difficulties that your employees are having. If you genuinely want to assist them by providing advice and help when needed—and you convey that intention—they will open up and share their burdens with you.

Part of what you can do for your employees is to be their advocate with higher levels of management. For instance, if you see, through your control process, that employees are struggling with outmoded equipment, you can ask your own boss whether the equipment can be upgraded. You and your staff make a team, and the more you can do to establish an atmosphere of close and supportive teamwork, the easier your job as a supervisor will be.

What Controls Would You Use?

Imagine that you're a supervisor for a large manufacturing company. One of your team's jobs is to produce a monthly inventory of parts on hand. There are 150 different parts to be inventoried, using data from six different departments. The task is especially important this month because your boss is going to make a major presentation about inventory controls to senior management.

Until now, the inventory has been done by Susan, but she has just been transferred to another department. Her replacement, Jayson, seems smart and dedicated, but somewhat touchy about close supervision; he likes to think he can handle things by himself. This will be the first inventory report he has done. The software he'll have to use is rather complicated, but he says he understands what to do. What kind of control process will you establish? Answer the following questions.

1. How will you monitor the accuracy of Jayson's inventory reports?

_____

_____

_____

_____

2. How will you keep track of whether Jayson is on schedule?

_____

_____

_____

_____

3. How will you check his motivation and morale?

_____

_____

_____

_____

4. How will you explain your control system to Jayson so that he understands it and cooperates with it?

_____

_____

_____

_____

- Three essential functions of a supervisor are: setting goals and planning, organizing the work and assigning tasks, and controlling work performance.
- Goals should be challenging but realistic, expressed in measurable terms, and set down in writing.
- Effective planning involves setting aside enough time to plan, clarifying priorities, dividing the tasks into small steps, and establishing a schedule for each step.
- Organizing the work requires successful delegation of tasks, and delegation works best when you transfer genuine authority and responsibility to your subordinates.
- Controlling is a regular, ongoing process of checking on quality, schedules, costs, employee satisfaction, and any other important aspects of the job.
- In all of these functions, supervisors have the greatest success when they communicate their reasoning to their employees and encourage the entire group to think and work as a team.

A lonzo is a new supervisor at a commercial printing firm, and his first three weeks have been relatively easy. This Friday morning, however, he has a tough call to make.

A local college—one of the firm's largest clients—is sponsoring an Alumni Weekend to celebrate the opening of a new science building. Alonzo's team has been working on a full-color, glossy booklet for the college to hand out tomorrow morning to the visiting alumni. The job was delayed while the college designers fussed with the details. Yesterday Alonzo sent out a final proof. The college was supposed to approve it by this morning, but no one from the college has responded.

Alice, the customer service person, has been trying in vain to reach her contact at the college. Alonzo knows that if the printing doesn't begin right away, there won't be time to finish during regular working hours. What should he do? He'd like to discuss the problem with his own boss, but Mr. Wallace is on vacation.

Alonzo's head swirls with the possible consequences of the wrong choice:

♦ If the booklets aren't ready on time, the college staff may be furious (even though the delay was their fault), and Alonzo's firm could lose a major client.

♦ If Alonzo starts the printing right now and the college doesn't like the results, that decision, too, could cost the firm a major client.

♦ If the college's approval comes in this afternoon, Alonzo could set up an overnight shift to finish the job. But Mr. Wallace might be angry about the cost of overtime wages.

Luckily, Alonzo has had some supervisory training. He sits down, takes a deep breath, and reviews what he knows about the process of effective decision making.

What's Inside

In these pages, you will learn to:

♦ deal with uncertainty and risk .... p. 38

♦ follow steps for effective decision making .... p. 41

♦ "sell" your decisions to others .... p. 45

Uncertainty and Risk

In Workshop 1 you learned that making decisions and solving problems is one of the key functions of a supervisor. You want both your employees and your superiors to  trust you to make the right decision at the right time. You can't be an effective leader if you're seen as indecisive or prone to mistakes.

Like Alonzo in the scenario you've just read, you may find that most of your decisions are simple and routine. Occasionally, though, you'll face a truly tough call. It may involve a touchy situation with employees, a tricky problem with a client, or a quandary in interpreting your own company's rules and guidelines.

What makes a decision difficult? Usually two factors are responsible:

♦ Uncertainty
♦ Risk

The way you deal with these two factors will greatly influence your success as a decision maker.

In the context of decision making, the term *uncertainty* means that you can't predict the likely effects of each possible outcome—or perhaps you can't even guess what the potential outcomes may be. Imagine that your production team is creating a video for an important client to present at a trade show. You notice a small, five-second flaw in the video. If you decide to fix the flaw, the job will be late. You don't have any previous experience with this client, nor do you know the precise date of the trade show. On one hand, would being a day late make a big difference in this case? On the other hand, would the client notice the small flaw? Would viewers at the trade show notice it, and what would happen if they did? In this situation you face a lot of uncertainty.

Risk means that there is some danger for you, your team, or your organization if you make the wrong choice. In our video example, your firm may lose a big client if you make the wrong decision. Your entire team's reputation may suffer. Personally, you may get an earful from your boss and damage your chances for promotion.

How can you best handle uncertainty and risk? Although each situation is different, these techniques often help:

♦ **Seek more information.** Additional information can reduce your uncertainty and help you calculate the degree of risk in each possible choice. In our sample situation, you might not want to tell the client about your problem, but you could ask other people in your

> " We are prone to say that an organization has done well because of exceptional leadership. What we generally mean is that the *decisions* taken . . . have been good decisions. "
>
> —Charles Perrow
> *Complex Organizations*

firm about the client's typical preferences. You could discover the date of the trade show. You could find out how the video will be projected and therefore how visible the flaw would be.

- **Ask for other people's opinions.** Your colleagues and your employees can be valuable sounding boards for your ideas. Even if the decision is yours and yours alone, it's no shame to consult others. They may help you see new ways of approaching the problem.

- **Involve team members in the decision.** Often, if a decision will affect the entire team, it's appropriate to call a meeting and let the team members help you decide. Your employees may even come up with options that you haven't considered. In our video example, maybe the team members will volunteer to work late to fix the problem and meet the schedule.

- **Make a fallback plan.** Plan in advance what you will do if particular risks materialize.

- **If the problem is too large, consult your boss.** Now and then, you may be faced with a decision that is too complex or too all-important for you to make without involving your superiors. If you approach your boss by saying something like, "We have a problem I think you ought to know about," you're not ducking your responsibilities. You're giving your own supervisor a chance to intervene or to offer guidance.

If I don't look, will the problem disappear?

Many of us approach difficult decisions by procrastinating. We behave as if a problem ignored long enough will vanish of its own accord. Sometimes the original problem does indeed disappear—by turning into a bigger one. A minor matter becomes a crisis.

Surely, you don't want to rush a big decision. Often you can "sleep on it"—that is, let your mind work on the matter overnight, or perhaps for several days. But there is a fine line between that approach and procrastination.

If you can acquire information to aid your decision, start doing that now. If you can consult other people, begin that process right away. Then, instead of just "sleeping," your mind will be making progress.

Uncertainty and Risk

How do you confront decisions that involve uncertainty and risk? To analyze your own typical approach, decide how well each of the statements below applies to you. Mark each item using the following scale:

4   Very much like me

3   Somewhat like me

2   Mostly unlike me

1   Completely unlike me

_____ 1. When I have to make a tough decision, I don't expect any help from others, especially not from my employees or classmates.

_____ 2. When I'm uncertain about a decision, I stop to figure out which facts I need and how I can get them.

_____ 3. In most decision making, I "shoot from the hip," trusting my instincts.

_____ 4. In a risky situation, I analyze the risk of each possible choice.

_____ 5. Even if I don't have a fallback plan, I go ahead.

_____ 6. I discuss difficult choices with others who are involved, seeking everyone's opinion.

_____ 7. I worry so much that I put off decisions.

_____ 8. I plan what I'll do if things go wrong.

_____ 9. I would never admit to my boss that I'm having a problem.

_____10. I'll listen seriously to advice from any reputable source.

To calculate your total score for this exercise, first *reverse* your scores for the odd-numbered items. On item 1, for instance, if you wrote a 4, make it a 1; if you wrote a 2, make it a 3. Now add up all the numbers.

The maximum score is 40. The closer you came to 40, the more likely you are to be successful as a decision maker. How close did you come? In what areas do you need to change your approach?

Steps for Effective Decision Making

Researchers who study effective decision making often break the process down into several distinct steps. Although you may not always be aware of these steps as they occur, understanding them can help you improve your own decision-making process.

Step 1: Define the Decision

"Defining the decision" may sound too automatic to need discussion, but you'd be surprised how often supervisors mislead themselves about the scope of their own decisions. Long-term, high-impact decisions have a way of disguising themselves as simple everyday choices.

Imagine that you've been assigned to head a team on which Gwen and Bill are the two senior employees. You don't know either of them very well, but in your first few days on the job, you find Gwen easier to talk to. Now you find that a sensitive task has to be done, and you don't have time to handle it yourself. You'll have to delegate it to Bill or Gwen. You're inclined to choose Gwen. You'd feel more comfortable with her handling the task.

But stop a minute. In this situation, you should ask yourself: "What am I really deciding here? Am I simply assigning one task? Or am I saying that Gwen is going to be my main assistant from now on?"

As another example, think of our earlier scenario involving the video with a five-second flaw. Say you decide to go ahead and finalize the job without fixing the flaw. Are you also deciding that, if someone notices the mistake, you'll pretend you didn't know about it? Do you really want to be a liar?

You'll be a better supervisor if you're self-aware enough to understand what you truly mean by the decisions you make.

Step 2: Explore Alternatives

Many decisions present themselves in an either-or format. Choose Gwen or Bill. Release a flawed video on time, or fix it and fail to meet the schedule. Often, however, if you think creatively, you'll realize that other options are available.

> If there is one quality that best describes a supervisor or a manager, it is that of being a decision maker and a problem solver.
>
> —Jack Halloran and George L. Frunzi
> *Supervision: The Art of Management*

Consider the either-or problem of whether to pick Gwen or Bill to handle a sensitive task. What might some other alternatives be? Here are a few:

♦ Call in Gwen and Bill and ask them to work together on the project.
♦ Call a meeting of the entire team and ask for suggestions and volunteers.
♦ Delegate some of your other work so that you can handle the sensitive task yourself.

Besides using your own ingenuity to explore alternatives, you can ask for suggestions from others—your employees, your boss, your colleagues. Don't trap yourself in an overly limited set of options.

Step 3: Analyze the Effect of Each Alternative

Once you have assembled all the possible options, you should investigate each one as logically and thoroughly as time allows. Think about both the short-term and the long-term consequences of each choice.

At this stage you often need to gather more information. To evaluate the options in our Gwen-Bill example, you might need to seek answers to questions like these:

♦ Has the team handled tasks like this in the past, before I became supervisor? If so, how? Who did what?

♦ Could Bill and Gwen work well together? Have they worked together before?
♦ Is there any mutual jealousy between them, so that one might be jealous if the other were given an important job?
♦ If I assign the task to one or the other, will they think my choice has serious implications for the future? For instance, if I choose Gwen, will she think she's my number-one aide? Will Bill think that?
♦ How do other teams in the company handle matters like this?

A little bit of information-seeking can make your decision a great deal easier—and smarter.

Step 4: Choose and Implement the Best Alternative

Once you've assembled the pertinent information and analyzed the alternatives, go ahead and make your decision. You don't want to fall into "paralysis by analysis."

Next, take appropriate steps to implement your decision. Choosing Gwen to handle a task won't do any good unless you give Gwen a full briefing, hand over the background data she will need, discuss with her exactly what has to be done and when, and tell others she has the authority to deal with this matter.

> " A supervisor should be demanding but fair. "
> —David Galli
> Metal Fabrication Manager

Step 5: Review the Outcome

A final step—too often ignored—is to take some time afterward to review the outcome of your decision. This step is important for three reasons:

1. If you find you made the wrong decision, you may be able to reverse it, or at least head off some of the worst consequences.
2. The outcome may create new problems that require new decisions, and the sooner you become aware of these, the better.

3. If your decision turned out poorly, you can profit by analyzing the reasons for your mistake. Ask yourself, "How could I have foreseen these negative outcomes? What can I do better in the future?"

? Did you know

When faced with a tough decision, many supervisors believe they can rely on their instinct or intuition. Sometimes they're right, especially if they are experienced managers with a deep understanding of human nature.

The foundation of good intuition, however, is prior knowledge and thought. If your "sixth sense" warns you that a certain choice is wrong, it's because your brain is processing relevant information from your past experience. Consequently, your intuition will improve if you work to establish a strong base of knowledge.

Practice Your Decision Making

Look back at the scenario on the first page of this workshop. Imagine that you are Alonzo, and apply the five decision-making steps to his problem with printing the college booklet.

1. *Define the decision.* State the decision to be made as precisely as you can. (If you think that the main choice involves other, unstated decisions, list those as well.)

   _____

   _____

   _____

2. *Explore alternatives.* Think of all the possible ways of handling this situation.

   _____

   _____

   _____

   _____

3. *Analyze the effect of each alternative.* Briefly describe the likely consequences of each choice.

   _____

   _____

   _____

   _____

4. *Choose and implement the best alternative.* Indicate your choice and describe your plan for putting it into effect.

   _____

   _____

   _____

   _____

5. *Review the outcome.* Is there anything you should do later to check on the outcome of your choice and try to learn from it?

   _____

   _____

   _____

"Selling" Your Decision

Supervisors often make their own lives difficult because they fail to "sell" their important decisions. "Selling" in this sense means convincing other people that the decision was the right one.

You may think: "If I'm the supervisor and the decision is clearly mine to make, why should I worry about convincing other people? They'll see the outcome, and then they'll know I made the right choice."

Maybe. But if you don't get key people to "buy into" your decision, any of the following may happen:

♦ Your employees don't see the importance of your choice, so they don't bother to do what you've asked them to do.

♦ Your employees think you're wrong, so they do the opposite of what you've specified.

♦ You get a reputation for "flying by the seat of your pants."

♦ Your superiors as well as your employees suppose that you were unfair or arbitrary.

♦ If the decision turns out to be wrong, everyone assumes you had no good reasons for making the choice you did.

♦ If the decision turns out to be right, you get less credit than you deserve.

To put the matter another way, you want to be right, but you also want others to agree that you are right. Perceptions do matter.

Walking around afterward to tell people how smart you were won't accomplish this objective. Instead, when you make an important decision, you should communicate not only the choice itself, but also your reasons for it and the degree of importance you are assigning to it. Let your employees know that you have thought the matter over carefully and taken everything into account.

Of course, this task will be easier if you've adopted a participative style of leadership, as described in Workshop 2. Employees who were involved in the decision-making process will already be well informed about the matter. Workshop 5 will return to the subject of employee participation in decision making, and Workshop 6 will tell you more about methods for communicating with your staff.

The Ethics Check

The easiest kind of decision to "sell" is one that is not only smart but ethical. If your choice involves, say, cheating a customer, your employees may go along in the short run, but they will lose respect for you, and your long-term authority will be undermined. And if you're dishonest about the factors underlying your decision, you may find that people understand your thinking far better than you would like.

Many companies have formal codes of ethics. If this is the case in your own company, abide by the code. You should also have your own code that goes above and beyond what the company requires.

When you're not certain about the ethical nature of a decision, try to take time for what the Edward Lowe Foundation calls a brief "ethics check." Ask yourself questions like these:

- Does this course of action fit company policy?

- Is it entirely legal?

- Will this choice build respect among my employees and colleagues?

- Do I have to conceal any of my thinking from my boss?

- Would I be ashamed to tell my friends about my choice?

- Would I be embarrassed if customers or clients found out?

- Will I think better or worse of myself?

Did you know

One of the best ways to convince employees to "buy into" your decisions is to accept accountability. That is, let people know that you stand ready to accept blame as well as credit for the outcome. When a decision goes wrong, don't try to pass the buck. Admit it was your mistake.

Once employees see that you can be trusted not to play the "blame game," they may work extra hard to turn even your dubious decisions into success stories.

A Decision from Your Past

Recollect a time when a supervisor, teacher, or family member made an important decision that directly affected your life. Answer the following questions about the situation.

1. Did the decision maker communicate his or her reasons for the decision in a way that you could appreciate and understand? How well did you understand?

   _____

   _____

   _____

2. How did the person's communication, or lack of it, affect your respect for the person (for instance, your feelings about his or her intelligence, reliability, and trustworthiness)?

   _____

   _____

   _____

   _____

3. How did the communication, or lack of it, affect your willingness to comply with the decision?

   _____

   _____

   _____

   _____

4. After reflecting on this experience, what lessons have you learned? How can you apply this experience to your own decision making as a supervisor?

   _____

   _____

   _____

   _____

GETTING CONNECTED

Many web sites offer information relevant to the topics of this workshop. For instance, for general tips on decision making, see

http://www.liraz.com/tdecision.htm

For articles on ethics in business, look at some of the online offerings of the Ethics Resource Center:

http://www.ethics.org/articles.html

Because identifying good alternatives involves creativity, it's also helpful to explore sites that offer tips for enhancing your creativity, such as these two:

http://www.jpb.com/creative/

http://www.directedcreativity.com/

WORKSHOP WRAP-UP

- Under conditions of uncertainty and risk, you can improve your decision making with techniques such as seeking more information, asking for other people's opinions, and involving team members.
- The steps for effective decision making include defining the decision, exploring alternatives, analyzing the effect of each alternative, choosing and implementing the best alternative, and then reviewing the outcome.
- To convince employees to support your decisions, be sure to communicate your reasons for your choices.

After two years of work for a large supermarket chain, JoAnn hears that she's being transferred to a new store, where she will become the day manager of the bakery department. It's a big promotion for her, and the store is in her own neighborhood, so her commute to work will be easy. But she is warned that the bakery's sales have fallen below projections, and she is expected to improve the situation.

Before she reports for work, JoAnn thinks about her own experiences with that particular bakery department. She has bought fresh rolls and cookies there, and they were just as good as in every other market in the chain. But one day last summer, when she stepped to the counter to ask about having a cake decorated for a friend's birthday, she waited several minutes before any of the employees took notice of her. They were too busy talking with each other in the back. When a person finally came over to wait on her, the service was brusque and not very helpful.

JoAnn's first few days as a supervisor confirm her suspicions. Although the bakery staff members try to look busy whenever she observes them, she can sense that they work because they have to, not because they want to. There's little joy in the employees' attitudes, and little pleasure in their exchanges with customers. No wonder sales are disappointing.

When she talks to the employees individually, they seem nice enough. They're not basically rude people. But they seem to have little desire to help customers.

"How can I motivate them?" JoAnn asks herself. "Salaries are good, working conditions are fine—what is missing here?"

What's Inside

In these pages, you will learn to:

Why Is Motivation Important?

The dictionary defines *motivation* as an incentive to do something. In a work setting, motivation is the internal drive that pushes an employee to perform at the highest possible level. In short, as JoAnn realized in the scenario you've just read, a motivated worker does the job because he or she *wants* to, not just because of the supervisor's orders.

Motivating workers, then, is one of your most important tasks. Highly motivated workers can:

♦ Increase production
♦ Improve quality
♦ Raise customer satisfaction
♦ Make the job as a supervisor much easier

Poor motivation can result in a lack of attention to quality, a failure to meet schedules, low output, tardiness, high absenteeism and turnovers, and a lack of concern about customer relations.

Types of Motivation

In the simplest terms, motivation stems from (a) desire for a reward or (b) fear of a loss or punishment. You've heard about "using the carrot or the stick," a saying based on ways to get a donkey to move forward. You can dangle a carrot in front of the donkey's nose—offering a reward if it does what you want. Or you can whack the donkey with a stick—a punishment for not moving.

Management experts believe that carrots are much more effective than sticks. If you think back to your childhood experience with rewards and punishments, you'll probably agree. Yes, punishment has its place—especially in deterring outright bad behavior. But punishment usually doesn't create a strong motivation to work hard at a task. In today's world, direct punishment is more likely to breed resentment and rebellion.

Your primary aid in building motivation, therefore, will be the rewards you can offer. What workplace rewards do you think are most important to people? You may immediately think of traditional rewards such as these:

♦ Increased salary and better benefits
♦ Higher status in the organization
♦ Greater job security
♦ Greater power and authority

These rewards are indeed significant for most people. A century ago, in fact, management theorists believed that little else mattered. Then came the Hawthorne experiments, which helped to change people's minds.

> "The only way you can motivate people is to communicate with them."
>
> —Lee Iacocca
> Former CEO of Chrysler Corporation

The Hawthorne Experiments

In the early 1900s, researchers at the Hawthorne plant of Western Electric, near Chicago, began a series of experiments on the effects of certain working conditions. The researchers divided employees into two groups. For one group, they increased the lighting level. For the other group, they kept the lighting the same. Then they measured the effect on the workers' output. The group with more light showed increased productivity.

The conclusion seemed obvious: more light in the plant would raise production levels. The researchers were confused, however, by the fact that productivity also increased in the group whose lighting remained unchanged.

To clarify the results, the researchers reversed the procedure. For one group, they dimmed the lights, while the other group kept the same lighting. What was the result this time? Again, both groups produced more!

At this point a team from Harvard University began a more elaborate set of experiments. Ultimately the researchers concluded that the crucial factor wasn't the lighting. It was the employees' psychological reactions. Workers involved in the experiments were gratified by the attention being paid to them. The increased attention was a sign, they thought, that managers cared about them and noticed the work they did. They felt more important.

Moreover, because of the way the experiments were set up, the employees had greater freedom from direct supervision. That meant they were more responsible for their own work, and they responded by working faster and harder.

Overall, the Hawthorne experiments alerted managerial experts to the fact that wages, job security, and other such traditional motivators were not the whole story. Workers seemed to want—maybe even require—something more.

What Motivates You?

To understand how to motivate your employees, you should reflect on your own chief motivators. Look at the following list and rank each potential motivator in terms of its importance to you. Circle the appropriate number on the scale of 1 to 5.

	Unimportant			Very Important	
Money	1	2	3	4	5
Recognition from coworkers	1	2	3	4	5
Participation in decision making	1	2	3	4	5
Health insurance	1	2	3	4	5
Status in the organization	1	2	3	4	5
Status among my friends	1	2	3	4	5
Personal sense of accomplishment	1	2	3	4	5
Belief in company's goals	1	2	3	4	5
Authority over other people	1	2	3	4	5
Recognition from management	1	2	3	4	5
Chances for promotion	1	2	3	4	5
Challenging work	1	2	3	4	5
Pride in my own work	1	2	3	4	5
Financial security for my family	1	2	3	4	5
Pleasant work environment	1	2	3	4	5
Pension or other retirement benefits	1	2	3	4	5
Loyalty to the company	1	2	3	4	5
Loyalty to my superiors	1	2	3	4	5
Interest in the work	1	2	3	4	5
Friendships with coworkers	1	2	3	4	5
Job security	1	2	3	4	5
Chance to realize my dreams	1	2	3	4	5

Now look back at the items for which you circled 3 or above. In the jobs you've had, have your supervisors recognized what was really important to you? How did their recognition, or lack of it, affect your work performance?

The Hierarchy of Needs

After the Hawthorne experiments and similar studies, experts on management realized that intangible human factors had a lot to do with employee satisfaction and motivation. In Activity 5.1, you may have assigned high priorities to items such as "personal sense of accomplishment," "pride in my own work," and "chance to realize my dreams." These factors are difficult to measure in any precise way, but they have a huge effect on motivation.

In the 1950s Abraham Maslow offered a theory that helps explain the importance of such factors. Maslow said that people are motivated to satisfy their needs, and those needs fall into a pyramid-like hierarchy (see the illustration below).

At the base of the pyramid are *physiological* needs, such as food, water, and shelter. In the next level are needs related to *safety and security*. A person's salary and benefits affect these two levels of needs. For instance, you can buy plenty of food and feel safe and secure if you have good wages and medical insurance. Similarly, safe working conditions help satisfy the safety need, and a sense that your job is stable helps meet the need for security.

The next level of the pyramid involves *social* needs. We need friendship, affection, and a sense that we belong in certain social groups. For most people, the work environment helps fill some of these needs.

Second from the top of the pyramid is the block for *esteem* needs. These include both self-esteem and the esteem of others. If your work helps build your prestige, self-confidence, and sense of worth, it contributes to the satisfaction of esteem needs.

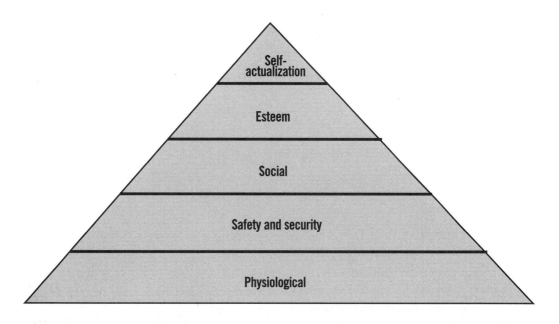

Maslow's Hierarchy of Needs

Self-actualization—or, to use a more common term, *self-fulfillment*—occupies the very top of the pyramid. This category refers to your need to realize your own potential—to achieve all that you imagine achieving and to be everything that you think is best. Perhaps this need is never fully met, but many people attain at least a partial sense that they have lived up to their own wishes for themselves.

In the pyramid diagram, notice how each level rests on the one below. Maslow believed that the lowest needs—physiological and safety/security—are the ones we seek to satisfy first. After all, we can't worry about fulfilling our potential if we don't have enough to eat. Once we meet those fundamental needs, we concentrate more on the social and esteem categories. If we're physically sound and secure, have good social relationships, and enjoy high status, we'll begin to think more and more about self-actualization.

What does the hierarchy suggest about motivation on the job? For people struggling to earn a living, salary and benefits may be extremely important, because these workers haven't yet satisfied their physiological and security needs. For employees who are better off, however, the subtler psychological needs begin to take precedence.

Now think back to the Hawthorne experiments. It wasn't the lighting itself that increased motivation and production, because the lights affected only the physiological setting. More important was the boost to workers' self-esteem that occurred when they thought managers were paying attention to them. And the sense of responsibility for their own work probably increased their self-fulfillment. These higher-level motivators were important in the Hawthorne plant in the early 1900s, and they are even more vital for today's workers.

Did you know

Most companies try to increase motivation by giving employees basic conveniences and a pleasant working environment—for instance, nicely designed offices, comfortable furniture, convenient parking. The assumption is that such benefits show that the company cares about its workers. In return, managers hope, employees will feel loyal to the company and motivated to do good work.

Notice, though, that these benefits fall into the lower levels in Maslow's hierarchy. They meet physiological and safety needs, but they probably have little effect on esteem and self-actualization. So how effective do you think they are as motivators?

What's the Need?

To assess your understanding of Maslow's hierarchy of needs, read the statements below and imagine that you heard a supervisor utter them to an employee. In each case, which kind of need would the supervisor be addressing? Some of the statements may relate to more than one need. Check all the boxes that apply.

	Physio-logical	Safety/ Security	Social	Esteem	Self-Actualization
1. "You're fitting in really well with your new team."	❑	❑	❑	❑	❑
2. "I'd like you to take on a decision-making role."	❑	❑	❑	❑	❑
3. "Your raise will begin with your next paycheck."	❑	❑	❑	❑	❑
4. "Are you free on Friday night? I have an extra ticket for the basketball game."	❑	❑	❑	❑	❑
5. "I've seen all the effort you're putting in, and believe me, we appreciate it."	❑	❑	❑	❑	❑
6. "Starting next month, we're setting up a pension plan."	❑	❑	❑	❑	❑
7. "You'll get a key to the executive washroom."	❑	❑	❑	❑	❑
8. "Do you have a minute to give me your thoughts on this problem?"	❑	❑	❑	❑	❑
9. "With your promotion, you'll get a larger desk."	❑	❑	❑	❑	❑
10. "I've written out general guidelines, but you can develop your own plan for the specifics."	❑	❑	❑	❑	❑

Motivating Today's Workers

In most industries, today's employees are better educated than in earlier times. They expect jobs to be interesting. They are used to having their opinions valued. They believe they are smart enough to make many of their own decisions.

Because of these employee attitudes, supervisors frequently need to appeal to the higher categories of needs in Maslow's hierarchy. Here are some guidelines for doing so:

♦ Treat employees as individuals. Learn which rewards are most important to each person.

♦ Whenever possible, allow employees to take part in setting goals.

♦ Seek out and respect your employees' suggestions.

♦ Give employees the authority and responsibility for a whole job rather than just a fraction of it. As you learned in Workshop 3, this style of delegation helps employees take "ownership" of the work.

♦ Let employees make their own decisions. For example, tell them what job needs to be done rather than exactly how to do it.

♦ Find opportunities for employees to be creative.

♦ Offer a variety of challenging tasks.

♦ Set up teams of employees to handle large tasks, solve problems, and make recommendations. Involvement with a team helps meet social and self-actualization needs.

♦ Constantly let employees know that they are important and what they do is important.

> " The more freedom you can give your competent employees in management decision making, the happier and more effective they will be. "
>
> —Warren Avis
>   Avis Rent-A-Car

Tips for Giving Rewards

In addition to appealing to higher-level needs, you can increase motivation by the style and timing of your feedback.

✓ Offer praise and recognition often—and in public.

✓ Give feedback promptly, as soon as possible after the performance in question.

✓ Be sure your rewards are directly related to performance, not to personal bias.

✓ Realize that employees may perceive the lack of expected reward or recognition as criticism. Saying nothing is saying something!

Quick Skills

Motivation in Review

To review what you've learned about motivation, answer the following true-false questions. Circle the appropriate letter for each item.

1. Motivation comes from outside a person.   T   F

2. With today's workers, punishments are less effective than rewards.   T   F

3. Most employees care mainly about how much money they make.   T   F

4. A job can be an important part of a person's self-actualization.   T   F

5. The working environment plays a relatively small role in satisfying
   social needs.   T   F

6. Assigning a job to a team tends to reduce individual motivation.   T   F

7. Most employees don't want to be burdened with problem-solving
   responsibilities.   T   F

8. Feedback is most effective when it is given promptly.   T   F

9. The Hawthorne experiments showed the importance of needs such
   as self-esteem and self-fulfillment.   T   F

10. To avoid favoritism, you should offer all employees exactly the
    same rewards.   T   F

1. F 2. T 3. F 4. T 5. F 6. F 7. F 8. T 9. T 10. F

Inc.com, the online site of *Inc.* magazine, offers a wide variety of readings on motivation. Go to

http://www.inc.com/

and enter the word *motivation* in the search window. You'll find articles about general principles of motivation as well as ideas for handing specific situations.

Another source is the Entrepreneurial Edge web site, sponsored by the Edward Lowe Foundation. Direct your web browser to

http://edge.lowe.org/

and type *motivation* in the search window. Read some of the articles whose titles look interesting to you.

WORKSHOP WRAP-UP

- Rewards are usually more effective than punishments in motivating employees.
- People are motivated to satisfy needs of various types: physiological, safety/security, social, esteem, and self-actualization.
- Today's workers tend to be motivated by higher-level needs such as self-esteem and self-actualization, rather than by a mere desire for money and security.
- To increase motivation, effective supervisors involve employees in goal setting and decision making, give them plenty of responsibility, offer a variety of challenging tasks, and provide frequent supportive feedback.

Justin is in charge of the online store at a small new software company. His team sets up web pages that the company uses to sell its products. Today, when Justin stops in to talk with a colleague, Yakov, he sees that Yakov is reviewing one of the web pages on his computer screen.

"You know," Yakov says, "if I were a potential customer, I'm not sure this presentation would convince me."

Looking over Yakov's shoulder, Justin begins to get upset. "Lisa set that up, and I told her yesterday that it was all wrong. We need those graphics to really pop. She was supposed to change the layout by this morning, but I didn't have a chance yet to check with her."

"Well, she's probably working on it," Yakov says.

"I don't know. I got the sense that she was resentful of my criticism. And when I sat down at her computer and showed her what I wanted, I'm not sure if she fully grasped the point."

"Maybe you need to go through it again, step by step."

"But she's incredibly smart," Justin says. "If she wanted to understand me, she would. You know, I praise her every time she does something great, which is practically every week, and I let her make important decisions, so I don't know why she should be resisting this simple request."

"Could the problem be," Yakov muses, "in how you communicated?"

Justin nearly shouts, "What do you mean how I communicated? I said the graphics had to be fixed. And I *showed* her!"

"Calm down," Yakov advises. "Maybe you should find out how *she's* thinking about the problem. Then you can discuss the changes you want."

What's Inside

Communication Problems

In Workshop 5 you learned about the importance of giving frequent praise and prompt feedback and allowing employees to make many of their own decisions. Justin, in the scenario you've just read, felt that he had followed those principles with Lisa, so he couldn't understand why she failed to react well to a little bit of criticism. What communication mistakes do you think Justin made?

In this workshop, you'll explore some of the typical communication problems that arise between supervisors and their employees, and you'll learn why good communication techniques are vital in today's organizations.

Listen, Listen, Listen!

The first step in becoming a good communicator is to learn how to listen. You may think that you already know how to listen, but many supervisors have more trouble with that seemingly simple activity than they realize. They may *hear* the words employees say, but that isn't the same as *listening*. True listening means paying full attention to every cue that is expressed—as well as the implications of what is *not* said.

For instance, if you give an employee instructions about a certain procedure, and he responds with a soft "Okay, I see," do you assume that he understood? Are you listening to the tone of the words? What does the shrug of the shoulders mean? Does his lack of questions indicate that he really did grasp the procedure or that he's afraid to admit he doesn't understand?

Good listening habits can tell you many things about your employees, such as:

- What they understand and what they don't.
- What and whom they like or dislike.
- What new ideas they have.
- How they feel about their working conditions.

Did you know

A generation ago, most corporations liked to place their senior managers in secluded private offices. The result was that managers tended to be isolated from their employees. The new trend is just the opposite—to design offices so that people of all levels bump into each other on a daily basis. This interaction encourages informal communication and the free exchange of ideas.

Top Ten Tips for Good Listening

Each situation is different, and each employee is different. Nevertheless, there are general guidelines that can help you become a good listener. Here are ten useful tips:

1. **Take time to listen.** Obviously there are times when you're too busy for extended discussions. But you need to set aside times when you can listen carefully to employees' problems, reactions, concerns, and suggestions.

2. **Let employees know that you're approachable.** Adopt an "open-door" policy. That is, communicate your willingness to hear what employees have to say.

3. **Demonstrate that it's safe to talk to you.** Make it clear that you are not judgmental and that you aren't looking to trip someone up. If an instruction isn't clear, you want to hear about it, and you won't blame the person for not understanding. Also show employees that you won't betray confidences.

4. **If people don't come to you, go to them.** Some employees may take advantage of your "open door" by approaching you with their concerns. Others will be reluctant to do so, for any of a variety of reasons (shyness, fear of being judged, unwillingness to complain about others, and so on).

Therefore, a good supervisor seeks out chances to listen to employees.

5. **Set up multiple means, both formal and informal, for communicating with employees.** Some employees are comfortable talking face to face. Others would rather send you a note by e-mail. Some will speak up during a formal team meeting. Others will reveal their concerns only in casual conversations around the snack machine. Make multiple possibilities available so that you hear from everyone.

6. **Pay attention to nonverbal signals: tone, vocalizations (such as "um," "uh," laughs, and sighs), body postures, and gestures.** Often a person will say one thing but signal nonverbally that the true meaning is different. For instance, "okay" said with a deep sigh does not really mean "okay."

> " It is the disease of not listening . . . that I am troubled withal. "
>
> —William Shakespeare
> *King Henry IV, Part II*

7. **Put aside your ego while you're listening.** Don't get defensive if an employee offers a criticism or complaint. It's not about you personally, it's about the work environment. Show that you're interested in hearing what's wrong so that you can take steps to improve matters.

8. **Avoid anticipation**. Don't jump to conclusions or assume that you understand a person's comment before he or she has finished talking. You may misunderstand, or you may discourage people from saying what they truly mean.

9. **Suspend judgment**. Don't decide on the spot whether the speaker is right or wrong. Wait until you have a chance to think the matter over.

10. **Use active listening techniques**. *Active listening* means taking an active part in the conversation to make sure you are grasping fully what the speaker is trying to say. Active listening involves techniques such as these:

    ♦ *Attending*. Focusing closely on the speaker and maintaining eye contact.

    ♦ *Paraphrasing*. Repeating what the speaker has said in your own words, giving him or her an opportunity to correct you if you have misunderstood: "You're saying that the procedure seems too complicated, is that it?"

♦ *Summarizing*. Offering an occasional summary of the main points made so far: "Let's see, you've mentioned three problems . . ."

♦ *Interpretation checking*. Stating your interpretation of what the speaker is conveying—both ideas and feelings—and asking if you're correct: "It sounds like you're upset that you didn't get earlier feedback on your handling of this project, is that right?"

♦ *Using clarifying questions*. Asking questions that attempt to make a point clearer or more explicit: "Are you suggesting we should change our procedures?"

♦ *Using probing questions*. Asking questions that encourage the other person to expand or elaborate on what was said: "I think I see the problem, but why do you think it happened?"

Evaluate Your Listening Habits

For each of the statements below, decide how often it applies to you. Answer according to the following scale:

4   Almost always

3   Often

2   Seldom

1   Never

_____   1.   People can trust me not to misuse what they tell me.

_____   2.   In a lengthy conversation, I look at my hands or close my eyes in order to concentrate on the words.

_____   3.   Though I try not to interrupt, I often find myself asking people to explain their ideas in more detail.

_____   4.   When someone starts to tell me something I already know, I save time by indicating I understand the situation.

_____   5.   I enjoy just chatting with the people I work with.

_____   6.   People know how to find me, so I rely on them to do so when they have something to tell me.

_____   7.   If people criticize me, I try not to get mad. Instead, I make an effort to understand the reasons for their complaint.

_____   8.   Smart people command my attention. With people who are less bright, I don't take their remarks very seriously.

_____   9.   If I feel unsure about how to interpret a remark someone makes, I ask if my impression is correct.

_____   10.   With certain people, I know what they're going to say before they begin.

To calculate your total score for this exercise, first *reverse* your scores for the even-numbered items. On item 2, for instance, if you wrote a 4, make it a 1; if you wrote a 2, make it a 3. Now add up all the numbers.

The maximum score is 40. The closer you came to 40, the more likely you are to listen effectively to your employees. How close did you come? In what areas do you need to improve?

Giving Instructions

Whenever a new employee joins your team and whenever a team member takes on different duties, you may find yourself giving instructions. The way you handle this responsibility will have a big impact on the performance of your team.

Because today's employees often participate in planning and decision making, some firms prefer to use the terms *coaching* and *facilitating* in place of *instructing* and *training*. The new terminology emphasizes the idea that workers need to find their own way to accomplish a task. The manager's role is to assist them in this discovery, rather than to provide rigid, lock-step directions.

Whatever name you give the instructional process, the following pointers can help you maximize your success:

1. **Before you instruct, be sure you know exactly what you want to have accomplished**. You'd be amazed at how many supervisors give directions before they themselves have thought carefully about the work.

2. **Explore the employee's prior knowledge**. Let employees tell you what they already know—or think they know. In that way, you'll avoid assuming either too much or too little knowledge, and you may become aware of misconceptions on the employees' part.

3. **Describe the desired goal, its importance, and the criteria for deciding when it has been reached**. From what you learned in Workshop 5, you can see that motivation increases when employees understand the importance of their work. Moreover, if employees know how to evaluate the results themselves, they are more likely to keep at the task until the criteria are satisfied.

4. **If a task is complex, break it down into separate stages and deal with them one at a time**. Most people don't learn to swim all at once. They learn how to kick their feet; how to move their arms; how to breathe. Similarly, you should allow your employees to learn a complicated process one step at a time.

5. **Use simple, clear language; avoid jargon**. Stick to terms everyone knows.

6. **Encourage questions**. Since you don't want employees to conceal their perplexities, you should do everything possible to convince them to speak up during the instructional process.

7. **Allow the employee to plan the details of the work**. Even in highly structured tasks, small variations are usually possible. Allowing the employee to plan the details will increase motivation. Besides, your

specific techniques may not work well for a particular employee. Imagine that you're a right-handed person trying to show a left-hander how to remove a bolt in a car engine!

8. **"Show" as well as "tell."** If a picture is worth a thousand words, a demonstration may be worth ten thousand.

9. **Whenever possible, give the employee hands-on experience and practice**. An employee can learn a lot by looking over your shoulder as you demonstrate a procedure. But the next step is to let the employee try the task. Allow plenty of time for practice.

10. **Adapt your methods to the needs of the individual employee**. Each employee may have a distinct learning style. One may learn best from detailed, step-by-step instructions. Another may absorb little until the hands-on stage. Still another may need charts and diagrams. Your employees also have different personalities and different backgrounds. Read the feature "Dealing with Diversity" and think about how workplace diversity will affect your communications with employees.

Dealing with Diversity

In our era, employees are more diverse than at any other time in the history of North America. They come from a variety of ethnic groups, races, nationalities, religions, cultures, social classes, and language backgrounds. In addition, there are more women in the workforce than ever before.

To be a good communicator, you should be prepared to deal with this diversity. For instance, you may need to speak differently to male employees than to females. If an employee is still learning English, you may have to change the terms you use. A young person may require a different approach than an older, experienced person.

Conveying Your Knowledge

Think of a particular sports or recreational skill that you have mastered, such as shooting free throws, riding a bicycle, or swimming with the butterfly stroke. Now imagine that you are going to train a complete novice to perform this skill. Use the lines below to plan your instructions. Make your entries as specific as possible. (For instance, the goal for riding a bicycle should be much more precise than "not falling off"!)

The skill: _____

The goal: _____

Criteria for judging results: _____

_____

_____

Stages of the task: _____

_____

_____

Instructions for one particular stage: _____

_____

_____

_____

_____

_____

_____

How easy did you find this exercise? Which aspects of coaching will you need to work on as a supervisor?

_____

_____

_____

_____

_____

Giving Criticism

No matter how skilled you become at coaching your employees, you will sometimes have to criticize their performance. Depending on how you convey your criticism, it can have positive or negative effects. The right style of criticism can not only help employees improve in the future, but also enhance your relationships with your entire team. The wrong kind of criticism can lead to lasting resentment and deteriorating performance.

You can probably recall incidents when you received criticism that you thought was unfair or overly harsh. How did it make you feel? What was its ultimate effect? Wouldn't you have done better if the critique had been more constructive?

Here are some tips for making your criticism constructive rather than destructive:

◆ *Address the behavior, not the person.* Don't say or imply that the employee is lazy or stupid. Instead, focus on the specific behavior you want to change.

◆ *Frame the issue as a mutual problem.* Rather than making the employee feel like a lone target, show that you're both trying to solve the same problem. Invite the employee to express his or her own perspective so that you can work together to find an answer.

◆ *Balance the negative with the positive.* By mixing in praise for what the employee did right, you'll get better results than if you merely stress mistakes.

◆ *Focus on the present.* Don't drag up errors the employee made in the past. Stick to today's problem.

◆ *Show empathy.* The word *empathy* refers to the ability to share the feelings of another person. Constructive criticism demonstrates empathy because it shows you care about how the other person is feeling.

> " New supervisors do not fail because they lack technical know-how; rather, they fail because they are unable to get others to work effectively for them. They lack good people skills. "
>
> —Alfred W. Travers
> *Supervision: Techniques and New Dimensions*

Timing, preparation, and setting also affect the success of your criticism. Add the following techniques to your repertoire:

- *Gather information beforehand to make sure your criticism is accurate.* Find out precisely what happened before you speak. Nothing irritates so much as criticism that isn't deserved.
- *Give criticism soon after the event, but not while you're upset about it.* Like praise, criticism works best if it's offered in a timely manner, while the behavior or performance is fresh in everyone's mind. But don't speak while you're agitated. You need to be calm and fair.

- *Praise in public, but criticize in private.* Your criticisms are between you and a particular employee. No one else needs to know. Embarrassing people is usually counterproductive.

Discouraging Words

Think how you'd feel if your supervisor began a comment on your work with one of the following phrases:

- "I know you're doing your best, but . . ."
- "I thought you understood better."
- "Nobody else has had this problem."
- "I can't comprehend why you did this."
- "If you look at this more carefully, you'll see that . . ."

How would you rephrase these comments to make them more constructive?

Communicating with Lisa

Look back at the scenario at the beginning of this workshop, in which Justin complains that his employee, Lisa, isn't following his directions. Help Justin improve his method of conveying instructions and giving criticism. On the lines following each statement by Justin, describe a better approach, including specific things he could have said and done.

1. "I told her yesterday that it was all wrong."

2. "We need those graphics to really pop."

3. "I sat down at her computer and showed her what I wanted."

The web site of eHow has a variety of short pointers on communication with employees. Go to

http://www.ehow.com/

and select the category "Finance/Business," then "Running a Business," and browse the available articles.

Another good source for information on communication and coaching is the Entrepreneurial Edge web site, already mentioned in Workshop 5:

http://edge.lowe.org/

To build your listening skills in particular, explore these two sites:

HighGain:

http://www.highgain.com/

International Listening Association:

http://www.listen.org/

WORKSHOP WRAP-UP

- Successful managers are good listeners. They seek out employees' comments and use active listening techniques.
- To give instructions effectively, you should describe the goal, break the task into manageable stages, use clear language, allow for questions and practice time, and let the employee plan the details of the work.
- To offer constructive criticism, you should address the behavior rather than the person, frame the issue as a mutual problem, balance the positive with the negative, focus on the present, show empathy for the employee's feelings, and make sure your comments remain private.

WORKSHOP 7

At a cable TV company, Sandy supervises the installers—the technicians who set up cable service in houses and apartments. Part of her job is to conduct performance reviews. She believes she is fair and straightforward. Today, however, she is troubled about the yearly review session she had yesterday with Zahida.

In the class for new installers that Sandy taught last year, Zahida was a star pupil. Sandy expected her to be a whiz at the job, and she has been— except that a lot of her customers call afterward with minor concerns. They wonder why the cable box is next to the flower bed. Or they say they don't understand the VCR hookup.

In the performance review, Sandy began by praising Zahida's technical expertise. Then Sandy came to what she called "the customer relations problem." She said, "Too many of your customers have been acting confused, phoning in with questions. With other first-year installers, like Mark and Jack, there aren't nearly so many calls. So you should take more time to explain how the system works, why

you've installed it a certain way, and so on. That's part of doing the job right."

To Sandy's surprise, Zahida became agitated. "Nobody warned me there were too many calls," she said. "And if the questions are trivial, why should it matter? You know, some customers think a woman can't do a technical job. You said my 'expertise' was great, but now you're judging me by what ignorant people don't know. That's unfair!"

Zahida was so unhappy that Sandy ended the interview abruptly, saying, "We'll talk about this when you're calmer." Sandy still believes her critique was justified, but she ponders how she could improve her evaluation techniques in the future.

What's Inside

In these pages, you will learn to:

Why Evaluate?

As a supervisor, you will make informal evaluations all the time. You'll judge how well employees are performing, and at times you'll need to communicate your conclusions to them and to your own boss. Perhaps you will also do formal reviews like the one described in the scenario you've just read. Many organizations schedule regular performance appraisals at least once a year. The results are put in writing and become part of the employee's record.

Such formal occasions can inspire dread in both employees and supervisors. Employees are anxious about having their faults pointed out. Supervisors dread having to explain how an employee isn't measuring up to expectations, and they worry that employees will resent being judged.

If evaluations are so painful, you may be thinking, why bother doing them on a regular basis? Why not save them for special occasions?

There are several reasons for regular performance appraisals:

♦ They make you take time for a thorough consideration of each employee's progress.

♦ They help both you and the employee identify problem areas and work out solutions before the difficulties escalate.

♦ They give you a chance to convey praise and admiration for the employee's accomplishments.

♦ They provide the basis for awarding promotions and raises.

♦ They allow you to describe your expectations for the employee's future performance.

♦ Employees who know where they stand can make more informed career decisions.

♦ If an employee must eventually be fired, the formal evaluations provide important documentation, helping the company avoid lawsuits and charges of unfairness.

Performance evaluations, then, are a necessary chore. No special technique can make them a delightful task. But if you work at improving your skills, you can avoid much of the mutual dread that accompanies performance appraisals. Most important, you can achieve an outcome in which both you and the employee feel that something useful has been accomplished.

> If [people] demand little of themselves, they will remain stunted. If they demand a good deal of themselves, they will grow . . . without any more effort than is expended by the nonachiever.
>
> —Peter F. Drucker
> *The Effective Executive*

Evaluating Your Own Evaluation

To be a good evaluator, you have to imagine how your employees feel about the process. Think back to a time when you received an evaluation at work or in school that was at least partly critical of your performance. Then answer the following questions:

1. In what ways was the evaluation accurate?

    _____

    _____

    _____

    _____

    _____

2. In what ways was the evaluation inaccurate, unfair, or incomplete?

    _____

    _____

    _____

    _____

    _____

3. What was the effect of the evaluation on your subsequent performance?

    _____

    _____

    _____

    _____

    _____

4. How could the evaluator have made the procedure better and more useful?

    _____

    _____

    _____

    _____

    _____

Guidelines for Evaluating Employees

Organizations use a variety of methods for employee evaluations. You may receive a form with just a few basic questions, followed by spaces for you to write out your comments in detail. Or you may receive a form that lists many separate categories, such as "quality of work," "ability to meet schedules," "cooperation with fellow workers," and so on. Perhaps the form will ask you to use a numerical scale or choose among ratings like "outstanding," "superior," "average," and "below average."

All of these formats have advantages and disadvantages. In an open-ended format, you can more easily describe the nuances of the employee's performance. However, it is sometimes hard to avoid subjectivity in writing—and later in interpreting—such evaluations. The more structured formats are easier to use and interpret—and possibly more objective—but they give less attention to the individuality of each employee.

Whichever format your organization asks you to use, you can benefit from following these guidelines:

- Explain the evaluation process at the time employees are hired. Tell them when and where evaluations will take place, what method of evaluation will be used, what performance standards will be used, and what will be evaluated.
- Make sure the employee knows in advance the performance standards he or she is expected to meet. One way is to involve employees in setting their own goals.
- If there are significant problems with the employee's work, he or she should have received feedback about them before the formal performance review. Try not to spring any surprises.
- During the evaluation process, involve employees in identifying steps to take for making any needed changes and improvements. This creates a more collaborative process and encourages employees to take responsibility for achieving goals.

The Sandwich Technique

Many successful supervisors conduct evaluation interviews with a method known as the sandwich technique. First, they stress the employee's strengths and accomplishments. Then they note any problems or weaknesses. Finally, they return to positive remarks, showing how the employee can remedy the problems and build on his or her strengths. By "sandwiching" the bad news between more positive remarks, the supervisors avoid overemphasizing the negative, and they convey their own solid support for the employee.

- Allot plenty of time to prepare for the appraisal interview. Nothing you say or write should be hasty.
- Be fully aware of what your organization will do with your written reports. In narrative comments, be especially careful of the words you choose. You don't want to give the wrong impression to managers who read the evaluations later.
- In analyzing an employee's performance, focus on process as well as outcome. That is, ask yourself not just what happened, but why it happened.
- Take full account of the experience and training of the employee. Was he or she properly equipped to do the tasks?
- Be as specific as possible in your remarks. Give examples. For instance, rather than saying "You've often been late for work," say, "You've been at least ten minutes late seven times in the last month."
- Review the performance, not the person. Some supervisors favor the people they like. Others try so hard to avoid that problem that they do the opposite. It's difficult to be completely unbiased, but you have to try as hard as you can.
- Discuss the good as well as the bad.
- Don't speak or write comparisons between one employee and another. You may think to yourself, "Janet is catching on much faster than Dave," but if you tell Dave he's not doing as well as Janet, you're asking for trouble.
- Try not to rely on what someone else has said about the employee in question. You want first-hand evidence, not hearsay.
- Review the entire time period in question, not just the most recent or most memorable events.
- In your meeting with the employee, allow ample time to review and discuss your comments.
- Choose a quiet and private place for the interview, preferably one where the employee can feel relaxed.
- Emphasize that the evaluation is designed to help the employee continue to grow and develop in the job.
- Encourage the employee to ask questions and seek clarification of your remarks.
- Ask the employee to suggest a plan for improvement or for developing further skills.
- Don't cut the interview short if the employee expresses anger or bewilderment about your critiques. He or she has a right to react to what you're saying.
- Try to end the discussion on a positive note, agreeing with the employee on new goals for the next evaluation period.

> "You have to respect your people and their abilities. In turn, you have to earn their respect; you can't command it."
>
> —Tim Riester
> President of Riester-Robb
> Advertising

Evaluating Sandy

Look back at the scenario at the beginning of this workshop. On the basis of what you've learned about effective evaluation, identify four mistakes that Sandy made and describe how she could have improved the process:

Mistake 1: _____

_____

_____

A better approach: _____

_____

_____

Mistake 2: _____

_____

_____

A better approach: _____

_____

_____

Mistake 3: _____

_____

_____

A better approach: _____

_____

_____

Mistake 4: _____

_____

_____

A better approach: _____

_____

_____

Disciplining Employees

At times, as a supervisor, you may face the unpleasant task of having to discipline an employee. Disciplinary measures often result from infractions of specific company rules. Discipline may also be necessary if an employee repeatedly fails to meet performance standards.

You set the basis for good discipline by making performance standards clear and seeing that all employees are familiar with company policies. These preventive measures are especially important with new workers. If, despite your best efforts to coach and educate your employees, you're forced to take disciplinary action, you will want to make that action as effective as possible. In fact, some management theorists insist that discipline can be not only effective but also positive, benefiting both the company and the employee. In the most extreme cases, positive discipline may be an unreachable standard, but the following sections will help you strive for that ideal.

Stages of Discipline

Discipline usually proceeds through a number of stages, from mild to severe, depending on the nature and frequency of the infraction.

Stage 1: Oral warning or reprimand. In many ways, providing an oral warning or reprimand is similar to offering criticism, and you should follow the same guidelines you read about in Workshop 6. For example, a warning should be prompt, accurate, private, and focused on behavior rather than on personalities. If the employee did not fully understand what was required of him or her, the reprimand should also include an explanation of the relevant rule or standard.

However, an oral warning or reprimand is often sterner than ordinary job-related criticism. It points out that further such behavior will not be tolerated. Often, too, an oral warning is documented with a written record.

Stage 2: Written warning. If the oral warning proves insufficient, the next stage is usually to put the warning into a formal document addressed to the employee. At this stage, penalties for the next infraction are specified. A copy of the document goes into the employee's personnel file, and other copies are distributed to the supervisor's boss and to the union representative (if any).

Discipline Versus Punishment

Discipline is not necessarily the same thing as punishment. Punishment simply means subjecting someone to a penalty. Discipline implies an attempt to correct or reform the unacceptable behavior. Properly used, discipline helps a person take responsibility for his or her own actions.

Stage 3: Suspension. If the unacceptable behavior persists after warnings, the next stage is often suspension without pay. The employee is told not to report to work for a certain period of time, and usually his or her wages are stopped. The employee is also warned that, if the behavior in question doesn't improve, the next step is dismissal.

In many cases, suspension is used as a temporary measure while the offense is being investigated. If the employee is cleared of misconduct, he or she is reimbursed for the lost wages.

Stage 4: Dismissal. Occasionally, an employee commits such an outrageous act that dismissal is immediate. Large-scale theft, for instance, or sabotage, or threats of violence to other workers—these could merit an immediate firing.

In large firms, however, most dismissals occur as the culmination of a long series of warnings and other measures. Because government laws and regulations protect workers from unjust disciplinary actions, corporations take great care to comply with the rules. Before a person is fired, many firms require that he or she

receive formal counseling in an attempt to solve the problem. Union contracts may also specify the conditions under which an employee can be terminated. The supervisor's own manager almost always becomes involved in the decision.

In smaller organizations, the internal requirements for dismissal may be less stringent. But employee-rights laws and government regulations still apply. A wise supervisor doesn't simply yell, "That's it—you're fired! Get your things and be out of here in five minutes!" Such hasty action is begging for trouble. A complaint of wrongful dismissal can entangle the firm with state and federal agencies and even with the courts.

Tips for Taking Disciplinary Action

The techniques for communication and evaluation that you've learned in this workshop and in Workshop 6 will help you make disciplinary actions as effective and positive as they can be. Here are some additional guidelines to remember:

Did you know

Some companies, dedicated to making discipline a positive experience, continue to pay employees who are suspended for disciplinary reasons. They want employees to spend the suspension time thinking about their behavior, not resenting their punishment.

- Investigate each disciplinary matter thoroughly. Talk with the employee and with others who witnessed the behavior in question.
- Make the discipline fit the crime. Harsh penalties for small infractions are counterproductive.
- Apply rules consistently.
- Be sure to follow legal requirements as well as company and union rules for due process.
- Keep complete and careful records.
- Be forthright about the disciplinary steps being taken and the reasons for them.
- Don't try to avoid firing an employee by harassing him or her into quitting.

ACTIVITY 8.3

Check Your Knowledge

To review what you've learned about employee evaluation and discipline in this workshop, answer the following true-false questions. Circle the appropriate letter for each item.

1. The sandwich technique involves surrounding negative comments with more positive statements. T F

2. Employees should be discouraged from talking back during their evaluations or disciplinary hearings. T F

3. It's the behavior that matters, not the reasons behind it. T F

4. For some grave offenses, immediate dismissal can be an option. T F

5. Regular evaluations are good for the supervisor as well as the employee. T F

6. If you have negative comments to make about an employee's performance, you should save them for the scheduled performance review. T F

7. Effective supervisors do not criticize one employee by saying that another is doing better. T F

8. Effective supervisors allow employees to propose their own plans for improvement. T F

9. Although you should comment on inappropriate behavior or substandard performance, you needn't embarrass the employee by bringing up specific examples. T F

10. Suspensions always involve a loss of pay. T F

1. T 2. F 3. F 4. T 5. T 6. F 7. T 8. T 9. F 10. F

For a brief background on the management science of performance evaluation, see

http://www.performance-appraisal.com/intro.htm

Employer-Employee.com has information about performance reviews and related aspects of managing employees:

http://www.employer-employee.com/

You can also find relevant articles under the heading of "Human Resources" at

http://www.bizzed.com/

The web site of Fair Measures Corporation offers a section on wrongful termination:

http://fairmeasures.com/

Finally, by entering terms such as *employee review* and *performance appraisal* in a search engine, you can find articles, forms, and policy statements from a huge number of organizations, as well as links to companies that sell performance-review products or services. Glancing at some of these sites may help you decide how to manage your own employee evaluations.

WORKSHOP WRAP-UP

- Regular employee evaluations are useful for both the employee and the supervisor.
- In evaluating employees, effective supervisors communicate clear performance standards, emphasize strengths as well as weaknesses, and encourage the employee to discuss the comments and create a plan for the future.
- Disciplinary measures typically progress through a series of stages, from oral warnings to dismissal, with each step carefully documented. If handled correctly, discipline can often be a positive activity.

Big changes are underway at Artown Hotel, which has been purchased by a large hotel chain. The lobby is being remodeled. A new restaurant is under construction. And Omar's housekeeping staff is in an uproar. Rumors of layoffs and other disasters are flying everywhere.

To squelch the hearsay, Omar calls a staff meeting. He's been assured that no layoffs are contemplated, he announces, and nobody will be transferred. Also, he has checked the new health plan, and it's just as good as the old one. That takes care of three rumors.

He goes on to point out that the remodeling should attract a more upscale clientele, resulting in larger tips for everyone. The new management does expect, he admits, that rooms will be cleaned and ready for guests earlier in the afternoon. That means the whole staff should strive for greater efficiency.

At this point an argument erupts between Sylvia and Josue, who frequently have trouble getting along. "What's the problem?" Omar asks them. Sylvia complains that Josue's habit of hogging the service elevator for his carpet-cleaning equipment delays everyone else.

"How can we be efficient in cleaning rooms," she grumbles, "if we can't get from one floor to the next?" Josue retorts, "People who aren't so lazy use the stairs." "Please, you two," says Omar, and he tells them to meet him later in his office. He ends the staff session with an appeal for teamwork. Afterward, he realizes that what he's just seen may be an omen: the staff's small disagreements may intensify because of the stress of change. He thinks about ways to make the transition period easier, and he tries to remember what he knows about handling conflicts between employees.

What's Inside

In these pages, you will learn to:

8 WORKSHOP

Managing Change

In the early 1970s, the title of Alvin Toffler's book *Future Shock* became a commonplace expression. It referred to people's difficulty in adapting to the rapid pace of change in modern culture. Today, technological and social developments are even more rapid than they were in the 1970s.

In business as well as personal life, changes often occur with dizzying speed. Many supervisors face situations like the one Omar encountered in the scenario you've just read. Reorganizations, mergers, software upgrades, new work rules, new team members—in some companies, it seems like the ground underfoot is always shifting.

A few people enjoy frequent change and adapt well to it. Most people, however, find rapid transformations unsettling. It's hard to feel calm and secure in the midst of a revolution!

As a supervisor, you'll discover that many of your employees need help in dealing with changes in their work environment. Here are some tips for assisting them:

♦ Begin to plan for the change as early as possible, and inform your employees well in advance.
♦ Explain exactly what is being changed and why.
♦ Discuss with your employees how the change will affect their lives.
♦ If possible, allow employees to participate in planning and/or implementing the change. As participants in the process, they will be more likely to accept the outcome— and they may have ideas that improve the results.
♦ Dispel unfounded rumors.
♦ Emphasize the benefits of the change.
♦ Be honest about what you know and what you don't know.
♦ When possible, introduce changes slowly, step by step, to allow employees to accustom themselves to the new system.
♦ Encourage employees to consult you about their problems and concerns.

> "People involved in the decision-making process are more likely to accept change and support new ideas."
>
> —Mary Kay Ash
> Founder of Mary Kay Cosmetics

Change and Motivation

Look back at the scenario at the beginning of this workshop. Imagine you're Omar, and you want to make sure the changes at the hotel have a positive effect on employee motivation. Suggest four specific methods you will use. (Hint: You can use the hierarchy of needs diagram on page 53 to focus on methods of appealing to different levels of needs.)

Method 1:_____

_____

_____

Method 2:_____

_____

_____

Method 3:_____

_____

_____

Method 4:_____

_____

_____

The Nature of Conflict

Rapid change in people's working lives creates stress, which in turn often aggravates underlying conflicts. But even in stable situations, conflicts can disrupt an otherwise harmonious team. As a supervisor, you should try to understand the basis of conflicts and manage them in the best interests of the organization and of the people involved.

Two Common Misunderstandings

As a first step in exploring conflict, let's clear up two common misunderstandings:

Misunderstanding No. 1: Arguments Are Conflicts

A disagreement, in itself, is not a conflict. Even a loud argument isn't necessarily a conflict.

A conflict exists when people have different goals and they see each other as blocking the achievement of those goals. Say that Barbara and Ray argue about the best marketing method for a new product. If each is pursuing the goal of increasing sales for the company, they aren't in conflict—they want the same thing, they're just differing about how to get it.

Conversely, a conflict can exist without any overt sign of disagreement. Ray and Barbara may be so deeply opposed that they quietly sabotage each other's work, though on the surface they're scrupulously polite to each other.

Misunderstanding No. 2: Conflict Is Always Bad for the Organization

Certainly, conflict can have many negative consequences. It can increase stress, undermine morale, reduce staff loyalty, and prevent the collaboration needed to do the job properly. But conflict can have some benefits as well.

In a dynamic organization, goals often contradict one another. Imagine that Barbara's job includes purchasing materials that Ray uses in his work. Barbara wants to save money for the firm by using inexpensive suppliers. Ray wants to be sure his work isn't compromised by inferior materials. Both goals are good for the company, and a certain amount of conflict between Ray and Barbara may help create a healthy balance between cost and quality.

Conflict can also help spark new and original ideas. It may spur employees to take greater initiative. It can help focus the staff on problems that need solution. Conflict that produces benefits of this sort is often called *constructive conflict*.

Your goal as a supervisor, then, should be not to eliminate conflict, but rather to manage it so that it becomes as constructive as possible, producing the most benefit and the least harm.

Three Keys for Understanding Conflicts

When supervisors mishandle a conflict, the failure often occurs because they didn't really understand what was going on. Three key principles can deepen your understanding of conflicts among your employees:

1. **Take full account of the personalities and backgrounds of the individuals involved**. Maybe Barbara and Ray are always having little spats—that's how they get along. In their case, it might be much more

Did you know

Most U.S. law schools now offer courses in dispute resolution, and hundreds of communities have centers where individuals and companies can seek help in resolving conflicts.

indicative of a conflict if they *stopped* sniping at each other. With some other employees, however, one sarcastic remark may be the sign of a deep conflict. You're likely to have all types of people working for you, and you need to be sensitive to their individual personalities.

2. **Look for underlying goals and needs.** Employees may not tell you precisely what they're arguing about; they may not even know themselves. Use your experience with them and your insight into human nature to discern their underlying desires and fears.

3. **Recognize the possibility of a "win-win" outcome**. Even when two people's goals seem mutually exclusive, there is often less opposition than you might think. For instance, Ray and Barbara may be in conflict over a promotion that only one of them can get. But if both of them value self-fulfillment more than mere status, there may be ways for both to feel satisfied. In a "win-win" outcome, both parties gain what they truly want, and neither feels like a loser.

ACTIVITY 8.2

Analyzing a Conflict

Think back to a two-person conflict you have witnessed in the past—at work, at school, or in your family. Then answer the following questions about it.

1. What was the conflict about on the surface? That is, what did the people say they were fighting or disagreeing about?

_____

_____

2. What do you think were each person's underlying goals and needs?

_____

_____

3. In handling the conflict, did both people manage to satisfy their goals and needs? To what extent?

_____

_____

4. With the benefit of hindsight, can you describe a healthier way of resolving the conflict—one that would have better satisfied the underlying needs of both people?

_____

_____

Resolving Conflicts Constructively

Not every conflict needs your intervention. Again, you should be sensitive to the particular individuals involved. Sometimes the best technique is to let them handle matters on their own. Ask yourself: Can they reach a solution by themselves? Will they settle the matter fairly, or is one person likely to ride roughshod over the other? Will they both remain committed to the job afterward?

In some cases, a private conversation with each person may be necessary. You can tell each party to the conflict that you're concerned about its disruptiveness and you would like to see it settled. That small intervention may give the employees enough motivation to resolve the matter.

At other times, however, you'll need to get deeply involved, sitting down with the parties to mediate a solution. In this event, the following techniques can help you resolve the conflict constructively:

♦ Make it clear that you expect the people to resolve their differences for the good of the organization.
♦ Encourage the parties to see the problem as a mutual one that they need to work together to solve.
♦ During the discussions, be sure they treat each other seriously and with respect.
♦ Urge them to express both their ideas and their feelings openly.

♦ State in your own words the issues and emotions involved, and ask both parties to correct you if you've misunderstood. Often, simply by reframing what they have said, you will put the conflict in a new light for them.
♦ When necessary, state your own opinions about what you've heard. You want to be fair, but that doesn't mean you have to be neutral on each point.
♦ Help the parties identify goals that they share.
♦ Taking the shared goals into account, press the employees to discover possibilities for a "win-win" outcome, or at least a compromise in which each gets part of what he or she desires.
♦ As part of the solution, lead the parties to define specific changes they will make in their behavior.
♦ Be sure both parties commit fully to the agreed-upon solution.

When you help employees work through such a collaborative, problem-solving approach to a conflict, the process often strengthens their relationship with each other and with you. In the long run, you may find that the conflict proves beneficial to your team.

> ❝ Conflict resolution is essentially a process of bringing a submerged issue out of the darkened waters and up to the surface where it can be seen. ❞
>
> —Brian Muldoon
> *The Heart of Conflict*

Reviewing Change and Conflict

To review what you've learned about ways to handle change and conflict, answer the following true-false questions. Circle the appropriate letter for each item.

1. In resolving conflicts, facts are more important than emotions.   T   F

2. Supervisors shouldn't scare employees by telling them about planned changes too far in advance.   T   F

3. A loud argument is not necessarily a sign of conflict.   T   F

4. Employees who participate in implementing change are more likely to support it and feel good about it.   T   F

5. Conflict can spur creativity.   T   F

6. Whenever conflict occurs, the supervisor should take direct measures to resolve it.   T   F

7. If potentially disturbing changes must be made, they should be accomplished all at once, instead of in dribs and drabs.   T   F

8. Identifying shared goals is a key step in resolving conflicts.   T   F

9. Effective supervisors try to eliminate all conflicts among team members.   T   F

10. Many work-related conflicts have "win-win" solutions.   T   F

1. F 2. F 3. T 4. T 5. T 6. F 7. F 8. T 9. F 10. T

GETTING CONNECTED

You can find a number of resources on conflict at the Conflict Resolution Network:

http://crnhq.org/

Resources on anger management can also be helpful for both you and your employees. One useful site is:

http://www.angermgmt.com/

The American Psychological Association's article "Controlling Anger—Before It Controls You" is available at:

http://www.apa.org/pubinfo/anger.html

WORKSHOP WRAP-UP

- Supervisors can help employees cope with change by being frank and open, inviting employee participation in the change process, and introducing changes one step at a time.
- Conflicts between employees can be either beneficial or harmful, depending on how you manage them.
- Constructive conflict management involves helping the parties see the situation as a mutual problem, express their feelings honestly, and discover "win-win" solutions.